THE
TEMPLE OF SOLOMON

A STUDY OF SEMITIC CULTURE

BY

PHILLIPS ENDECOTT OSGOOD

ISBN: 978-1-63923-602-2

Printed: January 2023

Published and Distributed By:
Lushena Books
607 Country Club Drive, Unit E
Bensenville, IL 60106
www.lushenabks.com

ISBN: 978-1-63923-602-2

TO

PROFESSOR KELLNER

TABLE OF CONTENTS.

LIST OF ILLUSTRATIONS.

INTRODUCTION.

I.

THE Temple of Solomon stands nearer the Red Sea than it does to Babylon. Its position is significant. For a few brief moments between the lessening chaos of the nation's genesis and the increasing chaos of the dissolution, the Temple is the permanent, fixed background of the drama of Jewish life; just as the never-failing temple façade of Mycenae provided the permanent scenery of the Greek theater, in whose fore-courts transpired all the action of tragedy and comedy.

A moment ago the Judges ruled, whose irregular succession runs back into the legendary morning-mist of Egypt and the Exodus:— a few moments yet to come and the "waters of Babylon" sweep in, and with their tide carry away all but the dream-shadow of the glory of the race. Solomon may have no place in the history of Jewish theology, but his reign marks a decisive instant in the history of Jewish religion, for he gave this house to Yahveh. Henceforth the Ark of the Lord abides no more beneath transient curtains, but has a central, permanent abiding-place in the midst of an Israel which is no longer a group of scattered hill tribes, living the patriarchal, unfederated life of the past, but a compact kingdom. Peace had come for the moment. The worldly life of the Hebrew nation was just beginning. The religion of Yahveh was coming into its own. The Temple becomes the precipitant and center of cohesion in the life of the Hebrews.

II.

It is a trite, safe statement to make that the religion of the Jewish people contained the possibility of truth and further revelation because it carefully and painstakingly abstained from any bias toward anthropomorphic limitation. The limiting of artistic life involved in the rigorous command that there should be no "graven images" in "the likeness of anything in the heaven above, the earth beneath or the waters under the earth" carried other limitations as well. Architecture, simple decorative design, esthetic perception of any kind was thereby stultified. By the fetters thus imposed on them the hands of the artist were paralyzed into the hands of the artisan, whose work henceforth inevitably must be totally devoid of anything but the faintest trace of grace or distinction. There are few more absolutely crude and hideous human creations than the clumsily daubed pottery of Judea, the almost sole relics of its artistic(?) endeavors. "Jewish art" is as nearly a contradiction of terms as can be found. The artistic horizon of the ancient Hebrew was made up of conventional flowers, mythic beasts (whose habitat, being pure fancy, *could* not be kept organic by sobering contact with reality) and the baldest of architectural lines.

Of course, it is a comfort to know that the ideal of Jehovah, thus not tied down to the level of anthropomorphic representation, was thereby delivered and made ideally free. Perhaps in the first place the fiat of prohibition issued psychologically from a subsense that the Hebrew blood *could* not produce anything ideal enough to be admired or creative of respect and adoration, however infinite the permission and opportunity. Its birthright-genius was aniconic; a capability for passionate devotion to an abstract ideal.

III.

Be all this as it may, however, human nature seems to have asserted itself, and attempted self-expression in concrete, if imperfect form was the ever-recurring heresy. It was the thing religion had most to fight.

Modern Bible study does not let us believe that the Yahveh-ideal was created full grown and perfect, and revealed to Abraham in his covenant or to Moses at the burning bush; to be no more improved upon forever and a day. Monotheism grew out of henotheism, henotheism out of polytheism. Yahveh was at first far from the all-powerful Lord of the whole world. He may soon have surpassed them, but he was blood-cousin to Chemosh and Baal. He belonged to the same polytheistic-henotheistic family. Abraham and his immediate descendants seem, even in the later, worked-over accounts, to have employed the same religious symbols and forms of worship as did the people of Canaan and Phœnicia, and the era of the Judges is the logical sequel to this time. Egypt, although it rebaptized the God of Israel, was not a sundering force in the form of his worship. As Abraham stories depict his erection of an altar wherever he made a residence, his "planting a grove" or pillar in Beersheba as a religious emblem; as Jacob's legend shows him twice setting up a great stone;[1] so, subtracting the point of view of later, more Puritan writers, the pet heresy of Israel in all the following years of the Judges and both united and divided kingdoms appears to be simple *reversion to type*. The gods of Syria, of Canaan and of Phœnicia were the obvious refuge for the child race of the Hebrews when Yahveh-worship transcended their capabilities, because there seems not to have been any *great* difference of quality in the worship of Baal and Yahveh until the spiritualization of the Deuteronomic code began to show.

In primitive races anthropomorphism is a forgiveable demand. Even to-day our most compelling conceptions of God, say what we may, must be in humanly finite terminology. The crime of worshiping other gods appears to have lain essentially in the treacherous desertion of that God who had made Israel his chosen people out of all the nations of the world; in the breaking of a covenanted troth with the supra-natural benefactor; in the not living up to the human side of the bargain; rather than in the about-face turn to the worship of a principle recognized as inherently evil. Even the later prophets and redactors, in their imaging the relation of the nation to Yahveh as a marriage relation, seem rather to lay stress in their frank metaphors on the desertion-element than upon the essential sinfulness of the new relation. It is the sin of breaking faith, rather than any sin of moral degeneration that is condemned.

The *elements* of the other worships abound in the worship of Yahveh himself. Ashera, pillars and other rude symbolisms permeate the earlier Hebrew faith. Yahveh has his seat in a burning bush, combining both sun and tree worship elements; the sacred bull appears in all sorts of new forms,—as cherub, even as the symbol of Yahveh himself; the serpent symbol trails deviously from the Garden of Eden through the wilderness into seraphic form and the Holy of Holies in the Temple, there to await Hezekiah's iconoclasm. In so far as Yahvism lifts itself above the spatial limitation of the symbol, that symbol is spiritualized and transcended. All the Semitic nations had passed from mere idolatry; Yahvism simply was the least limited by concrete symbolism to tangible finiteness. The gods of other peoples were hospitable and accepted newcomers to their pantheon, but Israel's Yahveh did not. Such new additions and infusions as did come in must do so as his attributes, not as separate entities. Breaking faith with Yahveh, as Yahvism grew

[1] Genesis xxxv and xxxviii.

spiritualized, meant, therefore, as I have said, a reversion to type. The sin of Solomon in worshiping at the "great stone" or high place of Gibeon,[2] in his building mounds ("high places") for Chemosh, the god of generation, and for Hercules-Moloch, the god of fire; in his second-childhood worship of Venus Astarte[3] is greater than the sin of those who in the lapses of the earlier Judges' period turned to Baalim and Ashtaroth[4] simply because it implies a greater reversion. The ideal has grown a bit farther away from Chemosh, Moloch and Baal, in that the conception of the covenant is a little more drastic; but the breaking troth with him who "abideth faithful" is still the sin. It remains for prophetism to make the covenant a pure and spiritual concept; to free it from the taint and tinge of commercialism and bargaining; to make the worship of the nation realize the moral content of its heritage.

The Temple building, then, was nearer the Red Sea than to Babylon. At the time of Solomon the elements of all-Semitic religion shaped its essence more than did any exclusive tendency toward the later, true religion. Messias-faith was from the very nature of the case an anachronism and impossible. The Temple of Solomon very apparently embodies the common elements of the entire Semitic pantheon. Even its aniconic nature is not absolute, nor is it unique. The Ark of the Lord, the brazen pillars, the cherubim, sacred palm-trees and the like, all show traces of their symbolic origin. In Egypt, in Phœnicia, in Assyria, the first germs of henotheism were quickening, bringing into first being the extension of the previous idea that the symbols merely incarnate the super-symbolic deity into the idea that the various deities in their turn are but the various manifestations of one who comprehends them all. That Moses, in the desert solitude of Midian arrived somehow at henotheism in simple covenant terms seems indubitable, however much we doubt the objective reality of the burning bush theophany. Such speculation can well have originated under the influence of Egypt, where this trend of thought already had most impetus. Here the confederacy of local cults, while proclaiming a certain modicum of jealous and even hostile independence one from another, was gradually, under the fire of political centralization and philosophy, unifying and fusing. This was done most of all by the discovery of points of similarity between the local godlets, who were thereupon pronounced to be merely different manifestations of the same deity. The time of David and Solo-

[2] 1 Kings iii. 4;
[3] 1 Kings xv. 23.
[4] Judges, ii. 10-19; iii. 6-7; v. 8; vi. 10, 25, 30; viii. 33; x. 6.

mon represents very little advance over the earlier stage, so far as religion is concerned. The advance in secular importance was great, but the time was not yet again ripe for reflection, when only theology can grow.

This may seem far afield from the Temple of Solomon, but it seems imperative at the outset, since the data is so almost completely inferential, to mark out the underlying temperament and ideas which were its ultimate foundation. It is hard not to believe that in the Temple we find the symbols of the *earlier* stages of Yahveh-worship, kindred to the *contemporary* worship of neighboring gods, who have not developed so far as has the outstripping Yahvism towards that henotheism, which in its turn, as reflection comes to those whose deeper insight made them truly prophets of the truth, grows into pure monotheism. It was a selective, natural process by which the Jews developed the religion which was forerunner of the highest; not an inhuman, because solely transcendent, revelation of a faith complete.

But in it we still find the marks of earlier stages. Whether or no the symbolism of the elements of worship germaine to all the Southeast Mediterranean world was conscious is doubtful. Nevertheless it seems sure that apostacy from Yahveh and the worship of a cousin god is little more than the singling out of one of the family characteristics, filling again with meaning a symbol which has its more meaningless place in the orthodox temple, the reversion to the separate deification of an attribute, now merely one out of several modes of manifestation of that God who has more nearly reached monotheistic, assimilating supremacy. The Temple comes at a transitional stage, where the past and the future still are linked in visible symbols of present use. Henotheism is emerging from mere monolatry into monotheism:—the belief in one God is beginning hazily to contain a moral element. The ideal of a just God has its birth.

Thus the significance of the Temple is not to be found in a rigid difference in quality from the religion of other Semitic nationalities, but rather in the degree to which the worship of the polytheistic deities elsewhere has here fused into the worship of a single, inclusive being, whose existence denied that of otherwise and otherwhere concerned powers not at all.

IV.

Little more can the Temple's significance be found in a cause particularly national.

There does not appear to have been any concerted, national

demand for a central shrine, no matter how glorious. The first centralization of the worship at Jerusalem was the cause, not the effect, of a powerful priesthood. It became a vantage point for further stringency and organization, but was not created by priestly ascendency. The national predestination to a religious rôle in history is not yet a compelling force.

The establishment of the Ark at Zion had given royalty a tinge of divine right. The king was Yahveh's lieutenant, the establisher and protector of Yahveh's abode. The disorganization of David's old age, when rebellious family quarrels strained the unity of the nation, succeeded by the growing alienation of the north;—all this furthermore precluded concerted action by the people in such a demand. Moreover, if the people were not enough united to think of centralizing their worship, neither were they discontented enough with their local "high places" to dream of abandoning them. This free worship in the open air was orthodox and precious to the pastoral commonalty, in heart half-nomad still. The essence of Yahvism seemed to be the *non*-localization of its worship. The local pastorate of the priests of the shrines, not a hierarchy at Jerusalem, was the desired thing. There was no innate necessity for a central shrine. Local "high places" were more compatible with the open country life, as well as with the growing disorganization of the nation.

Renan[s] claims that the Temple was nothing but the plaything of a vainglorious monarch, whose one idea in building it was the political aggrandizement of his dynasty, by making Yahvism thus theatrically appear dependant on the court. With his statement that it was not a national institution we may agree, but the imputation of mere vainglory may be needless. Solomon, however rapacious, capricious and tyrannical he may seem in the obviously unfriendly Bible accounts, need not have had at heart a selfish motive only. To label his motive "political" is not to brand it with the mark of Cain. It may have been the natural thing that his scheme of general and fitting stability and dignity for his government should include, as a matter of course, the building of an adequate house for the Ark. It need not have presupposed the negation of the validity of other shrines. The fact that it originates as a personal plan rather than as a national one does not prove it a selfish design. To make the conception of a fitting house within the confines of the capital for the symbol of Yahveh into a flaunting blazonry of regal mummery is unnecessary. The Temple may have been (as I think it was) a private court chapel in idea, and as such the most dignified seat of Yahveh's glory; but there are two possible interpretations of the fact. All that is required here, however, is to demonstrate the fact, *that the Temple was not created by a concerted national demand.*

This private court character of the Temple is little evidenced in the Biblical accounts.[6] But I Kings cannot completely have been compiled until about four hundred years after the death of Solomon, and Chronicles is at least three centuries later yet. By that time the Temple had the flavor of unrememberable generations of placid acceptance. As years went by, and the weakness of the court, combined with the strength of the priests and prophets, made the Temple the central, unique stronghold of true orthodoxy, the Jews forgot the primitive conditions; and, accepting the innovation, as its innovative character was swallowed up by the growth of custom, began to champion the Temple as the credential of their faith. The erstwhile protested shrine, by the very evolution of compulsory centralization, became the only valid House of Yahveh. The "high places" and all their open-air worship were looked back upon by later times with shrinking abhorrence, so that we naturally find the accounts of those more primitive times obviously colored by inability to enter into their mental equation. We read, therefore, that Solomon loved the Lord, "*only* he sacrificed and burnt incense in high places."[7] His subjects, too, might have been quite impeccable and orthodox ancestors if "*only*" they had not worshiped thus. The historian nevertheless finds enough charity to assign as the reason for this slipshod heresy the undeniable fact that "there was no house yet built unto the name of the Lord."[8]

If we can rid ourselves of the idea that the Temple was not yet nationally necessary we may appreciate the determined opposition of the simple fieldsmen, especially in the more nature-blessed and distant North with Ahijah the seer as their spokesman. Indeed, for the moment it must have looked like a retrograde step to house Yahveh within walls,[9] even though those walls were in the capital city and glorious with golden imagery. It was almost the same reversion to the limitations of type which in individuals constituted the outward garb of heresy. The essence of Yahvism demanded

[6] Yet no surprise is expressed when Absalom makes a vow to the Yahveh of Hebron; and Solomon's own regard for Gibeon, whatever palliation and excuse the author may assign in the lack of the Temple, is nevertheless despite the *Ark* in Jerusalem.

[7] I Kings, iii. 3.

[8] I Kings iii. 2.

[9] The shrine at Shiloh had doors, and Micah had a house for his image, but this seems not to have separated them from the class of sacred hill-tops, etc.

aniconic, natural worship. The remonstrance of those to whom court life meant little more than further arbitrary taxes, foresaw the future abolishment of even religious freedom in the present germ of the Temple, within whose courts orthodoxy most particularly would soon dwell.

V.

Modern Bible consciousness is prone to place the level of this era's civilization much too high. The Temple, as must be iterated and reiterated, was nearer the Red Sea than to Babylon. It represents a relatively primitive period. Worldly profane importance was in its brief zenith, but the true rôle of Judaism was just beginning its growth into strength and individuality. Spiritualization lay ahead, gained by storm and stress, by disappointment of the secular aim, by prophetic work to do.

It is not in any way a belittling of Judaism's truth to find in what period of that truth's evolution we for the moment are, and perhaps to recognize that it was not yet quite so perfect as at first we thought.

This distinctly comparative stage gives two preliminary presuppositions as basis of more technical data. They are these, as above suggested:

1. *Judaism embodies a religious genius as yet not unique.* In spite of the superiority over neighboring faiths which comes to the worship of Yahveh from its dawning henotheistic monotheism, there are common elements still retained throughout, proclaiming blood-relationship with the rest of the Semitic world, however polytheistic it may be.

2. *The Temple is not created by an essentially national demand, to whose unique genius it must rigorously conform.* Solomon himself (or David) is the one by whose initiative the Temple was built. Although in later years it came to be the accepted central shrine of the people; at the time of its construction it was a court shrine, built to house the Ark.

The first premise permits analogy and inference to be drawn from those elements in other Semitic religions whose relics are archeologically sure, wherever in the Temple or in Judaism there are data with which organically to connect them; since Yahveh worship gives ground for such community of ideals and elementary symbolism. The second in its turn still further widens the field on which to draw, since Solomon's own desires were the impelling force, not national prejudice. It allows us to look for plans and architectural skill outside of Judaism, which could itself so ill supply them. By this is not meant that the Temple becomes non-Jewish, but that there is not as yet exclusiveness in its source.

While these two principles have been called presuppositions, nevertheless the argument to come must largely depend for its strength upon their reenforcement, as hypotheses capable of cumulative verification. The reasoning, I frankly admit, is more or less circular, but must necessarily so be.

PHOENICIA.

I.

THERE are two centers of civilization in the Mediterranean world in the earliest reaches of history—Egypt and Assyria. Greece was not yet established as the third and apex angle of the old world culture-triangle. Egypt and Assyria (which includes in its generic type Chaldea and Syria) developed, as the outcome of their national individualities, distinctly national arts. They were the motive powers of the inner life-currents of all the rest of the Eastern Mediterranean. Not only the products of art as art, but her products as evidential manifestations of religion traveled backward and forward. But neither Egyptians, Chaldeans nor Assyrians had need or desire to hawk their own goods. Yet their products have been discovered, as far west as Spain (O. T. "Tarshish"), so middlemen there must have been. Whether it was predilection or the stimulus of geographical location that made the inhabitants of Phœnicia the traders and merchants of the era we cannot tell; yet either actually or through their colonists they had an almost complete monopoly of the carrying trade of Asia and Africa. Driven by events which we know only in their effects, as early as the twentieth century B. C. this people had established itself on the narrow strip of coast at the foot of the Lebanon range. They were thus half way between the Nile and the Euphrates, and within easy reach of both. By the time of David and Solomon they were an established state of many centuries standing. From Tyre and Sidon especially, but also from Jaffa, Acre, Gebal and Hanath, auxiliary cities of this one hundred and twenty miles of narrow coast, fleets of vessels sailed continually over all the basin of the Mediterranean. Cyprus was Phœnicia's colony; so probably was Crete.[10] Even as far west as Carthage in North Africa and Tarshish in Spain the intrepid traders established "coaling stations" for further sailing. Forms and motives

[10] This is, of course, after the power of the Minoan kingdom had been annihilated.

invented in Egypt and Mesopotamia were carried to foreign and then barbaric races, who in turn adopted them as bases for their own genetic culture. The shrewd merchants soon grew rich as heart's desire. Factories employing hundreds of artisans turned out figurines, pottery, metal paterae, dyed fabrics (especially of Tyrian purple) and jewelry by wholesale tonnage; all on Egyptian or Assyrian models. The native countries could or would not supply them conveniently, cheaply or fast enough for exportation and dissemination.

Judging, however, from Phœnician monuments and relics as known to us to-day, it seems that these trader-manufacturers were sterile in art of their own. They lacked creative genius; were powerless to make new art. Their skill lay in the manual dexterity with which variously borrowed types and derived ideals were mingled. The mixture was Phœnician, but the elements were Assyrian and Egyptian. In historic comment or in extant relics their *skill* is everywhere evident, *but their genius was obviously mechanical, adaptive and distributive; not national or creative.*[11]

II.

That Solomon continued a friendship and alliance which his father had established, we are assured by the Bible accounts and re-assured by historic probability. Tyre was next-door neighbor to Jerusalem; Solomon was a man of peace; Phœnicia was a friend to every one (with an eye wide open for business as the by-product of her friendship). Judah, too, was now a well-organized kingdom, small according to modern standards, but then reckoned moderately large. The Egyptian alliance had enough strengthened Israel's prestige to make it worthy of Hiram's deep respect.

Furthermore the similarity of the Phœnician language to the Hebrew shows in its almost merely dialectical variations a common bond, apparently of origin and blood.

But in the historical and prophetic books of the Old Testament it is not difficult to see that the Phœnicians exercised more influence upon the Hebrews than the Hebrews did upon the Phœnicians. It is the Jews, not the Tyrians and Sidonians, who, for instance, borrow names, rites and images from the other, despite the vehement expostulation of the prophets. It is Tyre, not Jerusalem, that is represented as offensively potent. The current of influence flows into Judea out of Phœnicia, not the other way.

Tyre, recently separated from Sidon, was in the full zenith of her power in the time of Solomon. Egyptian domination was a thing of the past;—Assyrian still of the future.[12] Since 1100 B. C. Tyre had led the way among Semitic countries in temple-building, basing its architecture mostly on that of its recent overlord; for Phœnicia's style was forever chameleon, changing to Egyptian, Assyrian or Greek coloring as its master changed. By now its Beth-elim[18] overlaid the little island of Tyre, the great central shrine of Melkarth predominant among them. Within eye-shot of the shore on a clear day, Cyprus likewise shone with buildings sacred to Phœnician gods.

Fusing historic probability with the Bible hint of aid in Solomon's construction, and also with the admitted inability of Jewish art to produce a temple so distinguished as probably this was, the conclusion seems to a high degree inevitable that its architectural form as well as artisan, skilled construction was supplied by Phœnician guidance and direction. I heartily believe that Hiram, king of Tyre, supplied the plans and specifications for the Temple at Jerusalem, as well as the wood and labor; as he, not Solomon, was competent to do. If they met with Jewish court approval as sufficiently dignified and magnificent, there could be meagre objection from a source which could not supply plans one-half as good.

This conclusion is further certified by the apparent resemblance of the type of architecture Phœnicia produced to the general impression we get from reading the accounts of the Temple at Jerusalem in the Old Testament itself.

III.

Modern archeological discovery in Phœnicia, Cyprus and Crete is almost entirely confined to grave relics. These small paterae, vases, pieces of jewelry etc., are naturally the means of very little information about architectural matters. They provide an ever-growing fund of material for the study of the religion and culture of the periods they embody, but the background setting of the life they indicate is still murky and obscure. The study of Phœnician architecture is predominantly analogy and inference; none the less legitimate perhaps, but nevertheless incapable of the tangible verification actual monuments elsewhere supply. "The very ruins have

---

[12] The Assyrian power began to reassert itself in the 9th century B. C. It was under Ashurnasirpal that the Euphrates was crossed and all northern Syria came under Assyrian domination (876 B. C.). Cf. *Keilinschriftliche Bibliothek*, E. Schrader, I, pp. 50 ff.

[13] בתאלים = temples. Cf. Phœnician inscription of the Piræus; *Revue Archaeol.*, Jan. 1888, pp. 5-7.

perished." The few buried fragments that have come to light date
from a much later period, when Greek influence had begun to mould
the supple skill of Phœnicia to its liking.[14]

The coast of Tyre and Sidon is the only field of pure Phœnician
relics; and there the dearth is most nearly absolute. In Cyprus the
additional element of Hellenism is apparent, but it is an unfused,
separable quantum in the finished whole, just as Egyptian and Assyrian motives remain distinct, though side by side, in earlier main-
land finds. In Crete the relics of Cnossos and its period are pre-
Phœnician and of a different genius. In Mycenean and post-Mycenean
relics the early Greek genius is paramount, yet there are those elements in its art which are inexplicable from within it unless we remember that Crete was once a Phœnician colony; perhaps without
much patriotic feeling for its overlord, but submissive to its com-
mercial, manufacturing dictates. Cretan discoveries go back to so
early a date that common bonds with Asia and Egypt through Phœnician and pre-Phœnician intermediacy are the necessary hypotheses.
This is particularly true in the relics of its most primitive religious
form, of its *betylae* (sacred pillar-stores), its tree-worship etc.,
which are found in every country reached by the influence of this
trader-nation. Of these symbols, this imagery of sacred stores, of
mythic and sacred animals, of sacred trees, there is much to be said
in connection with early Hebrew ideals, but to its later, proper place
such study of these communistic elements must be deferred.

On a number of coins of the Roman provinces of Cyprus, Per-
gamum and Sardes, on a certain number of gems, rings etc., there
are representations of a definite temple-type, whose specific embodiment as given is the Paphos temple of Astarte-Aphrodite. These
coins are late (all A. D.) and unless the type they represent can be
connected with much earlier examples they go for little. Also the
laxity with which architectural types are treated on coins, combined
with the limitations imposed by the meagre space at the engraver's
disposal, gives wide room for diversity of interpretation. Clearly,
however, we need not assume that the later, more elaborate types
are evidence of more complicated buildings, but rather is the obvious explanation increase of skill.

The Temple of Astarte (Venus-Urania, Mylitta or Isis) at
Paphos was the oldest and most honored holy place of ancient times.
As the nature-goddess, the embodiment of the secondary principle
in generation, the all-mother, her worshipers, though acknowledging

her under diverse names, traveled from far and near to reach this
her most famous shrine. Its origin is lost in fable-times. By the
day of Homer and Homeric songs its supremacy is famous.[15] According to Pausanius its prototype was in Assyria, i. e., in Babylon;
Herodotus[16] tells of a second possibility in Askalon, which latter
seems more probable, since Assyrian influence on Phœnicia was
much nearer Pausanius's day than to that of the Paphian temple's
construction. Its date is likewise misty and based on legend. Euse-
bius in his *Chronikon* sets it contemporary with Pandion I, king
of Athens, who was at least as early as 1900 B. C. All that can be
ventured with any show of probability is that the earliest Phœnician
colonists in Cyprus were the founders, in a time when racial lines
were not yet beyond fluidity.

The site of old Paphos is at Kouklea, about ten miles from New
Paphos. The oldest name for this is Golgi,[17] apparently a Phœnician
word akin to the Hebrew Gilgal.[18] In the Ptolemaic period old
Paphos was the site of the temple. Excavations in its neighborhood
have brought to light antiquities of all periods from late Mycenean
to Roman, but the age of the Temple must go back still further.
In the Roman period New Paphos became the capital and the coins
were issued thence; but it is the temple of *old* Paphos which is
represented on them. The flavor of its great antiquity was the
best advertisement New Paphos could put forth.

It is a reasonable presumption that when in 15 B. C. the earth-
quake destroyed their city[19] and Augustus came to the aid of the
Paphians, that some restoration was effected at the temple, and that
the shrine on his coins is the restored building. But it is at the
same time doubtful whether he would have made the restorations in
any but the pattern of the temple as it had stood so many years
before the mishap. Obviously too, if he had ventured to remodel the
temple in any but the ancient type, whose ancientness was its chief
recommendation to authenticity, he would have used the style of
architecture practised by Rome itself, not the (to him) foreign
native type of some other land. As we see it on his coins the

---

[15] Odyssey, Bk. Θ (VIII), l. 362, and Hymn in Venerem, l. 58.

[16] Herodotus, Bk. I, Ch. 105: "I have inquired and find the Temple at Ascalon is the most ancient of all the temples of this goddess, for the one in
Cyprus (Paphos) as the Cyprians themselves admit, was built in imitation
of it." (Ascalon = 40 miles from Jerusalem. Cf. Judges, i. 18; xiv. 10; also
cuneiform inscriptions of Sennacherib, 3d year.)

[17] Pausanius, VIII, 5.

[18] גִּלְגָּל

[19] Cf. Dion Cassius, Bk. 23 and Obermüller, *Die Insel Cypern*, p. 150.

temple is certainly neither Greek nor Roman but of a genius all its (Phœnician) own.

This type of temple is further authenticated as ancient by the golden models of a shrine found in the royal graves of Mycenae (Fig. 1). They are apparently very early, at least as early as the

Fig. 1. GOLD BAS-RELIEF FROM MYCENAE.
Schliemann's *Mycenae*, fig. 423.

twelfth century B. C. and approximate the Paphos representations so closely that it seems legitimate to conjecture that the Paphos shrine is their original, existing practically unchanged until the time of Augustus's renovation.

Therefore, whether the Roman coins we have represent the old or the new temple it makes little difference, since we are justified by its type in tracing back to Phœnicia as its original source.

These coins are no two alike, but the variations are not fundamental and are easily explicable as due to variations of skill, or different schemes of diagrammatic depiction of the same type. The simplest, commonest form, perhaps, is that given below (Fig. 2). Here we merely have two pillars bound together by cross-pieces, a semicircular forecourt, through the simple porch the cone of the goddess surmounted by her sacred dove, and on either side of the uprights conic symbols akin to that within. Between this and later coins the degree of complexity varies much, but these here-given elements persist.

The highest uprights seem to be modified Egyptian pylons. Across the top is often draped what seems to be a garland of flowers, though it is barely conceivable that it is an awning. The flanking cones are omnipresent, being the advertisement of the femininity

Fig. 2. COIN OF PAPHOS.
Gerhard, pl. XLIII, 17. Perrot and Chipiez III, p. 270, fig. 262.

of the deity within. Later they are also often represented as candlesticks, with flames at the top; which may perfectly well have been their utilitarian adaptation in later times. Their significance as analogous to Jakin and Boaz I discuss later. There seems to be an open court beyond the porch, in whose midst stands the sacred image, symbol of the goddess. Tacitus remarks that this image was never wet by rain, although in the open air.

In an engraved mirror from Cyprus (Fig. 3) this structure is repeated. But here the flanking cones apparently are brought within the court; their places outside being occupied by circular-topped uprights, which, nevertheless, are of the same feminine symbolism, being either the *omphaloi* of the goddess Astarte or the moon-disk of the Egyptianized Isis-Aphrodite. Later days may easily have transposed the flanking cones nearer the central object, leaving more definitely collateral emblems outside the fane.

In accordance with the usage of die-engravers of imperial times, the type is probably a combination of façade and section. Its architectural treatment suggests that its upper parts, at least, were made of wood, which may explain the difficulty of establishing any relation between the representations we have and actual remains. The still further articulation of this same thing is shown on the reverse of a silver coin of Vespasian (69-76 A.D.) (Fig. 4) whose later date and larger size allow greater accuracy of constructive drawing. The combination of façade and section is more clearly apparent; it suggests that the sacred cone stood in a rectangular court, whose

Fig. 3. ENGRAVED MIRROR FROM SALAMIS. THE TEMPLE OF PAPHOS.
A. P. di Cesnola. *Salaminia*, p. 59, fig. 56.

pylon faces us, its Egyptian resemblance being clear. Here we have side wings shown, at the expense of the usual obelisks. The sectional character is best shown in these side wings. They suggest a colonnade of slender pillars of which we see two, surrounding the courtyard; the windows at the extreme sides may possibly indicate circumferential rooms. Above the cone it would appear that an awning (running from front to back) or arrangement of garlands was hung. But the generality of representation at hand puts garlands across the tops of the pylon-uprights (cf. Fig. 2); if these are garlands they are most peculiarly and inefficiently placed, while

an awning is most naturally to be expected for shade, if not for protection from the rain; especially since we know both Egypt and
Assyria used awnings much, and Phœnicia's fabric-manufacture and
dyeing was rich and skilful enough to be worthy such a place for
its product.

In spite of the cross-beams, which are easily interpreted as

Fig. 4. SILVER COIN OF VESPASIAN (reverse). THE TEMPLE OF
PAPHOS.
British Museum Cat., pl. XV.

porch-lintel only, the construction behind must have been hypaethral
(open to the sky). Even in the elaborate representation of the
very latest coins and gems, when there is a metope-like construction
shown above the cone, there is no sign at all of a roof above the
central portion. The wings give the whole structure a superficial
resemblance to the primitive (and therefore Phœnician-influencing?)

Fig. 5. THE BRITISH MUSEUM GEM.
British Museum Cat., Greek Coins of Cyprus, pl. XXV. Fürtwangler,
Ant. Gemm., pl. 64.

Cnossian fresco at Mycenae, which was also constructed mainly of
wood.

In the British Museum Gem (Fig. 5) where an extra storey
is added, the side wings have a further growth. The date may be
later, but at least the gem shows that the three-storied chambers
of Solomon's Temple can be combined with an open-court shrine.

This open court is clearly indicated here by the awning above the cone.[20]

But most clearly of all, a coin of Byblos (Fig. 6) showing the temple there, shows the open court arrangement. The porch-like building on the left can readily be subtracted as the accretion of a later age; but the portion on the right has no resemblance at all to architecture other than Phœnician. The cone is not the sort of steeple the imperfect perspective ability of the die-cutter makes it look at first sight, but is in the center of the open space, around which a very obvious, though inebriate, peristyle is shown. The addition of rooms outside the peeristylar court would be in perfect keeping with the possibilities of the type, although this shrine need not have had them.

Fig. 6. COIN OF BIBLOS. EMPEROR MACRINUS, 217-218 A. D.

From Donaldson, *Architectura Numismatica*; also Perrot and Chipiez *Hist. of Art in Phoenicia*, Vol. I, fig. 19.

The pseudo-Lucian,[21] whose credulous account of the Syrian goddess contains a description of this temple or one in its close vicinity, mentions many details not given on the coin, but supplies us with nothing more believable than the story of the two pillars (Priapi) "standing in the porch"—believable, that is, if we take of the height he assigns a tithe at most. Probability reassures us of their presence. But when he labels the form of the temple he describes "as those of Ionia," that same probability laughs at his pedantic erudition; for the only Ionic forms that penetrated Phœnicia were *details,* which late accretions (such as Ionizing capitals and metope-façades) affected the generic nature of the architecture not at all. Its genius remained unchanged throughout all its history, yet that

---

[20] This does not seem to be the moon-crescent of the goddess, for its ends are attached to the pylon-uprights at the sides. The sitting doves are symbols enough to show whose is the represented shrine.

[21] *De Dea Syria,* (pseudo) Lucian.

type itself was by its very nature in essence nothing but composite. In the formula by which the heterogeneous mixture was made homogeneous lay Phœnicia's knack.

IV.

So much for the general outlines provided by such pictured relics as can be connected with our argument. Now for the meagre deductions to be gained from the few actual ruin-fragments. Most noticeable of all characteristics to-day is the colossal size of the stones used in the walls. This may be seen in the excavations of the foundation plateau of the Jerusalem Temple, as well as on the sites of Paphos and other Cyprian temples. But this argues nothing of the construction of the actual shrines within the walls, whose detailed ornamentation and manipulation would demand finer stone construction. We have also seen above that the coins suggest a light structure, possibly of wood in parts.

The calcerious tufa of the Phœnician territories is not susceptible of delicate ornamentation; so other material had to be used to supplement the lack. Casings of wood or of metal are the obvious inference, though almost all signs of such have disappeared. In the curved volutes and leafy decorations of (later) Cypriote capitals we seem to recognize motives suggested to the ornamentalist by the malleable elasticity of bronze. Added to this indirect evidence, one or two small sections of bronze sheathing have been found,[22] though again dating from a later period. From the Biblical accounts we also hear more infallibly of sheathing, where the overlaying metal and wood covered all the interior so that not a bit of stone-masonry was visible. So far as we can tell Phœnicia's architecture was based on Egyptian models. Certainly the "Tower of Babel" style of the Assyrian temples exerted no plastic force over Tyre and Sidon shrines. Egyptian forms, simplified for reasons of economy and ability, were decorated with largely Assyrian motifs; this was the method of hybridization. The result was severe in its ensemble, elegant in its detail. "Smooth walls very carefully built, friezes of carved and gilded wood, chargings of bronze, pictured symbolic animals and trees in vigorous polychromy and rich hangings fused in a unique and picturesque result."[23]

So far as minute decorative details go, I shall leave them as data for the minutiae of the temple of Jerusalem itself.

[22] Cf. Perrot and Chipiez, *Phœnicia.*
[23] Cf. Renan, *History of Israel,* ad loc.

EGYPT.

IF the main lines of Phœnician temples are Egyptian, there may be some data in that same source tending toward the clarification of Solomon's Temple.

The ancient empire of the ten Memphite dynasties left no temples of type analogous to that in hand, their very great antiquity being naturally concomitant with more primitive formlessness. The middle empire, with the capital at Thebes, leaves hardly a trace of its architecture as relic of the great and strenuous history of that evolution which culminated in the Hyksos Kings' supremacy. It is the Sait empire (21st to 30th dynasties) that has left us most of what survives to-day, although the later Theban dynasties (Rameses II was of the 18th) seem to have worked toward the Sait style. Since it is not until Sheshonk I[24] that we get contemporary with Solomon's day, it is permissible to use the temple of the new empire alone as the prototype of Phœnicia's adaptations.

The temple of the new empire seems to be marked by nothing so much as by complexity. A simple example is hard to find. When a temple was complete in all its parts, any monarch who wished his name to be perpetuated there, simply added a new building to it, which addition could only be a replica of some part already standing. Indefinite accretions give us the apparent complexity of Karnak.

But a simple example is most surely found in the temple of Khons[25] (Fig. 7) whose simplicity seems to have been left untouched from a very early date (Rameses III?), though in the near neighborhood of the great temple of Karnak itself.

First of all, the temple proper of Egypt is enclosed by a high wall which serves (1) to mark the external limits of the temple, (2) to protect the sacred place from injury and (3) to act as a

[24] His accession was 980 B. C.

[25] So used by Perrot & Chipiez (*Egyptian Art*, vol. I) and Lenormant (*Temple de Jerusalem*) e. g., pl. 19. (a cross section).

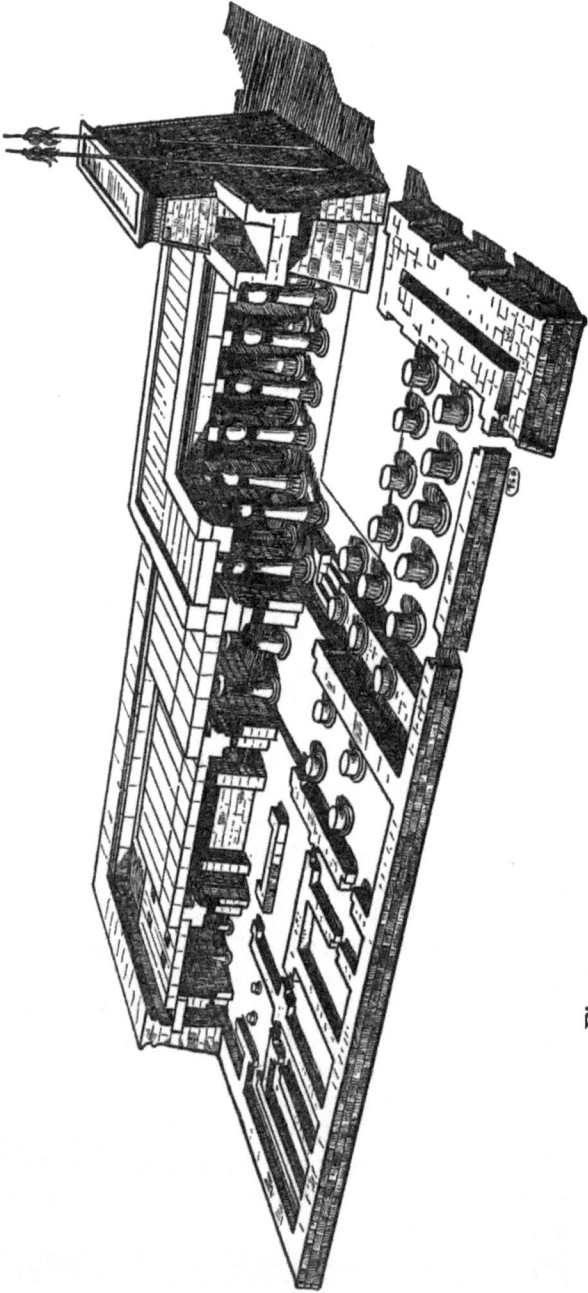

Fig. 7. THE TEMPLE OF KHONS: HORIZONTAL AND VERTICAL SECTION. From Perrot & Chipiez, *Hist. of Ancient Egyptian Art.* Vol I, fig. 208.

curtain between the curiosity of the profane crowd and the holy mysteries within. Avenues of Sphinxes lead up to the gateways from far away. Within the gates begins the sacred enclosure,[26] within which all religious ceremonies are performed. The temple proper may or may not have such honorable and majestic fore-courts. Khons has no outer wall at all; Karnak has four successive courtyards to be crossed before the shrine is reached.

The universal form of gateway is the *pylon*, whether it be in the walls (pro-pylon) or in the temple building. A pylon is of three parts. (A) a tall, rectangular doorway flanked (B and C) by a truncated, pyramidal mass on either side, rising high above its lintel. The object is purely ornamental, the outer and inner faces being profusely carved in low relief with scenes representing the monarch as the friend of the temple-god. Inside, the pylons are partly hollow; access to the small chambers is by means of ladders (in the earliest examples) or by winding stairs about a central, square newel (in the later).

In front of the pylon generally stand two obelisks, a few feet away from the base of the pyramid-masses; and, in really complete temples, just behind the obelisks and in contact with the pylons sit colossal statues of the king. To two obelisks there may be four or six statues. The obelisks extant vary from sixty to a hundred feet in height and the statues from twenty to forty-five. The pylon and its decorations thus compose the entire façade of the temple.[27]

Behind the *portico* comes a rectangular *Peristylar court*. The colonnade is of a double row of columns in front of a solid (sloping) wall. From this court a doorway leads into a hall of little depth, but of a width equal to the whole temple, whose roof is supported by close-set columns. This *Hypostyle hall* corresponds to the *Pronaos* of Greek temples. It is the "Hall of Appearance," into which only kings and priests are allowed to penetrate. The outer "Hall of Assembly" must suffice all others. The hypostyle hall is so thickly set with pillars in some of the larger temples that little, if any, vista is possible. This comes from the limitations imposed by stone slabs as roofing material.

Behind the hypostyle hall, there is a rectangular chamber, separated on all its four sides by a wide corridor from small chambers which fill in the space left vacant. This chamber we easily recog-

[26] Called the τέμενος in Greek temples.

[27] In the temple of Khons there are neither obelisks nor statues, but whether this is due to the minor importance of the temple, or to the removability of such small-sized relics as would be here proportional, it is not possible to tell.

nize as the *"Holy of Holies,"* the *"Cella"* of the shrine.[28] Fragments
of a granite pedestal have been found here, upon which must have
been placed either the "bari" or sacred boat, as often figured in bas-
reliefs (see Fig. 8) or some other receptacle of the emblem of the
local divinity.   Strabo tells us with surprise[29] that there was no

Fig. 8. THE SACRED BOAT (BARI) OR ARK OF EGYPTIAN GODS.
From Marriette-Bey, *Dendérah*, Book IV, pl. 67 and 68.

statue of the divinity here; but there must have been something to
distinguish it from the less sacred parts of the building, and the
identification of this something with a little shrine is patent.   It is
therefore far from guesswork to find in Egypt the prototype of at

[28] Strabo names it the σηκός.
[29] Strabo Bk. XVII, I.

least the Ark for which Solomon built the Temple, and the thought of a Holiest Place therein where the sacred chest should rest.

The smaller rooms round about must have been used as subsidiary chapels for consort and subsidiary gods, and for store-room and treasury purposes as well. They are indefinitely multiplied in larger temples.

Such was the basic idea of the Egyptian temple. Its details I postpone until I come to the Temple at Jerusalem, where some of them are of possible use.

THE TEMPLE OF SOLOMON: DETERMINING CONSIDERATIONS.

I.

THE actual reconstruction of the Temple at Jerusalem is incomplete without some slight idea of its setting. In the adornments of his capital, Solomon included the Temple within the citadel, his castle. The group of structures thus included comprised not only the king's residence, the palace for his chief wife, the daughter of Pharaoh (built in Egyptian style that she might feel at home?), the apartments of his other wives, but also a magnificent hall of audience for state occasions,[30] a smaller hall of judgment and the Temple (cf. Fig. 9). There seems to be no doubt left as to the site.[31] It is known in the Old Testament both as Zion and Moriah; in modern times as the Haram esh Sherif. In all probability it had been David's citadel, now enlarged to take in more of the hill for the accomodation of Solomon's more comprehensive and impressive massing of buildings. The natural unevenness of the ground was largely overcome by filling in the lower places, with retaining walls such as Herod later built. The enormous number of laborers required to "build the Temple" expended most of the seven years ascribed, not on the comparatively small building itself, but on the wonderful masonry substructure necessitated to raise the plateau to the level of the Temple court. Probably as much as one-third of the hill had to be built. The artificial plateau must have numbered at least fifteen acres. To-day it rises eighty feet above the debris,—debris so great that the bed of the Kidron has been moved laterally eighty feet and raised forty. Excavations have shown it to reach to the depth of twenty-five meters. The foundation stones thus exposed are well finished, showing they were originally in

[30] The House of the Forest of Lebanon.

[31] There has been much controversy between the advocates of the western and the eastern hills, but it seems to be settled in favor of the western one by excavations (Wilson and Warren) which show the substructure intact.

view. The method of their finishing is that called "rusticating,"
i. e., the main surface of the stones is left rough, but the edges are
sunken and smoothed, so that when the blocks are *in situ* the joined

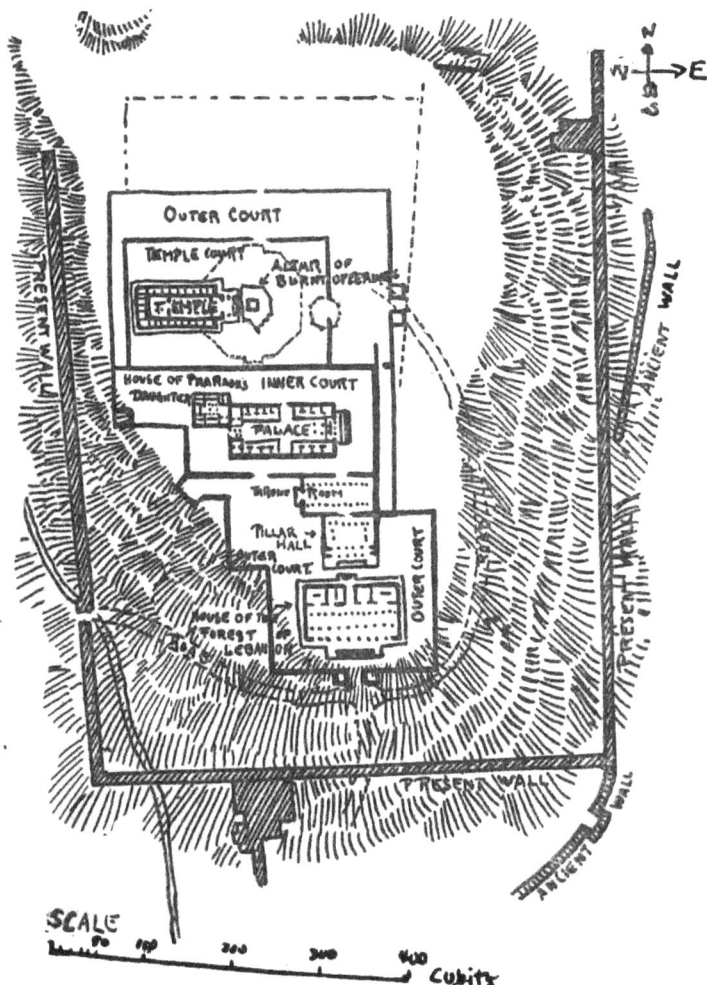

Fig. 9. MAP OF SOLOMON'S CITADEL.

edges form shallow, sunken channels. But this is a method of
stone-dressing it is hard to carry further back than the time of
Herod.[32] The enormous size of the blocks,[33] reminding one of

[32] The red vermilion marks on the bottom stones cannot be defined as a
dated Semitic alphabet, but are probably mason's marks.

[33] Some of them weigh at least 100 tons.

those in the wall of Baalbek, is remarked upon by Josephus of Herod's temple. Solomon's substructure, if anything, goes yet deeper.

The natural unevenness of the hill cannot, however, have been entirely overcome, for constant usage speaks of "going up" from the palace to the Temple. The Temple must have stood at the highest point, with the palace lower down to the south, and still lower the houses of the town. The sacredness of hill-tops is common to all Semitic religions. So we are justified in assigning this native summit as the original reason of its consecration. Probably we may go further and say it was already consecrated to the *genius loci* before David captured the city, in which case Yahveh simply adopted the locality; as at Gibeon, a Canaanitish town, he had displaced the local Baal, or become merged in him. This was no unusual process.

That the threshing-floor of Araunah the Jebusite had been within so short a step of David's palace is hard to believe, especially since the palace must have been the highest fortified point in Jerusalem. The site of Solomon's Temple could not have been determined by this. It is natural to suppose that the Temple gradually attached to itself legends originally concerned with other sanctuaries and that this is one such. Solomon built his court chapel in the citadel near his palace. As a hill-top it may have been sacred, but mere convenience of location, as better lending itself to the scheme of the whole, must have been the determinant motive of its situation.

II.

The scantiness of information concerning Solomon's other buildings seems to be for the sake of giving space to the description of the Temple. Some may claim that the description of the palace etc. represents about the true quantum of the knowledge the writers really had and that whatever accuracy and description of glories goes beyond that quantum in the Temple-depiction is invention, pure and simple. But difference of estimate would be enough to make the Temple bulk larger in their eyes than any palace buildings, since they wrote from a pietistic standpoint. The Temple, even while it remained an innovation, was of cardinal interest.

In the Old Testament there are three accounts of the Temple:

(1) 1 Kings v-viii. This leaves out much that is absolutely essential to a clear understanding of the structure, using technical terms whose meaning seems to have disappeared as completely as

has the Temple itself. Attempts to reconstruct their contents must always be attended by a high degree of uncertainty.

The last important event known to the author is in the latter part of the exile, making it therefore entirely possible to doubt whether the writer had any first-hand knowledge of what he is describing here. Yet the ground work of Kings seems to have been a more or less contemporary compilation from the archives, later worked over into our present form. At any rate the text is very corrupt as we have it, and needs careful emendation. There is, probably, a residuum of first-hand knowledge as the kernel of the account, but it is so overgrown with traditions as to the cost of the materials, the number of laborers, gold plating, etc. that little reliance can be put on anything not elsewhere duplicated.

(2) 2 Chronicles ii-vi. This is the latest of the three versions of the Temple description. Chronicles, however sincere may have been the spirit of the compiler, was written from the point of view of a Jerusalem priest sometime after the return, whose one idea was to glorify the past and make the true Israel seem as orthodox three hundred years earlier as in the priest-ruled, restored nation. David is therefore represented as having received the plan of the Temple from Yahveh himself; and the long description of the Temple is filled with little but the enumeration of the costly gold and brass, and the skill which decorated it. With no first-hand knowledge, the Chronicler doubles or quadruples measurements, exactly as his priestly, orthodox, and esthetic eye would like to have seen the original Temple.

(3) Ezekiel xl-xlii. In this alone do we get apparently first-hand knowledge. Ezekiel had been a priest in the Temple before the Exile. Probably it had changed little from Solomon's day, however much its ritual and significance to the nation had altered. The vision of the Temple which the prophet saw on the banks of the river Chebar must have been based more or less upon the actual, though now destroyed, Temple in Jerusalem. His visions are full and exact, and enable us to fill in many gaps in the other accounts ; but at the same time we must remember that this passage describes an imaginative temple and is not hampered by facts if Ezekiel's ideal is otherwise. Besides, how much of the dimensions of his church can even the most long-settled minister remember, once away from it for years? Ezekiel may be our best authority for the reconstruction of Solomon's Temple, but even he is pitifully inadequate.

Secondary references may be found in Josephus and the Rabbinical *Tract Middoth*, but these are both so based on Herod's Temple as to be worthless, unless in some few points where we need them not at all.

Our information is small, both documentary and monumental. "Historic probability" is the best guide. And this can be so variously twisted that it is small wonder an amateur museum might be stocked with the diverse ideals and reconstructions it is used to justify. I do not claim to have found the solution which will set the discussion of Solomon's Temple at rest; my claim is to add to the collection a reconstruction I have not been able to find, but which seems just as probable as any. Certainty is happily beyond the reach of any man.

III.

I take my major problem first. Was there a roof on the Temple? So far as I know, its existence has not been doubted. The Old Testament accounts have seemed to take it for granted. Modern consciousness seems to think one necessary to every building, ancient or modern. Yet, despite all this, I have ventured to doubt the existence of the roof in this present case.

(1) *Historic Probability.* The section on Phœnician temples had an ulterior motive; i. e., to show that Phœnician architecture did not contemplate a roof when concerned with temple-building. But the conclusion grew by simple study of the data, not from preconceived intent to be original. The endeavor to prove that the type of architecture depicted on Paphos coins (Figs. 1-5) was identical with that which was contemporary with Hiram of Tyre, so noted as a temple-builder, gave the basis for the claim that both were hypaethral.

Phœnicians did not build hypostyle courts like those of Egypt, for they were unable to afford such luxuries. The Phœnician genius was adaptation, and adaptation always omits that structural portion which is not essential to the *idea*, especially if at the same time that portion happens to be the most difficult one to reproduce. In Phœnicia there was no proper stone out of which the necessary roofing material could well be made. To be sure, on the Egyptian temple there was a covered court, but this was the very portion that was least essential to its idea. The hypostyle hall was so thickly set with pillars (because of the shortness of the roofing slabs) that the congregating of any number of people was out of the question; ritual itself was banished to the outer, peristyle court. The hypostyle hall served its purpose well. It was put there to act as a screen, pure and simple; to keep the gaze of the vulgar and curious from the sacred oracle of the god. The hypostyle court was the implement by which the taboo-separation was enforced. Phœnicians had two alternatives in their adaptation if they did not care to copy slavishly and lose that precious modicum of originality upon which they seem always to have insisted (perhaps unconsciously), so that Phœnician gods were trade-marked as such, though their motives, likely enough, were frankly borrowed. The first alternative was to cover in the whole court, i. e., to enlarge the "cella" until its mystery should compass the whole shrine and leave the openness of the outer court enough for all the popular worship. The other was to keep the shrine small, perhaps to reduce it to the god's symbol only, (though small chapel-like shrines of tiny size have been authenticated as the center of the open-courted temple) and to increase the open space by making one more courtyard intervene before the shrine;—that is, the central object (in whatever form) being the "Holiest Place," whether the next outer concentric circle of impression should be a mere enlargement from within of the same quality of building, sacred and mysterious, or whether it should be something more definitely marked from the point of view of the incoming worshiper as an approach *to* that sacred presence. It is natural that the question should be decided in favor of the simpler open court, doubly so when the deities of the nation were so simply embodied in rocks, trees, and posts, and the "Holy Place" of the god or goddess was reduced at its very core to a simple cone, uncovered by vestige of mystery. If precedent probability does not require a roof, neither does the evidence of subsequent architecture. For we are certain that, if Solomon's Temple had a roof, it was an engineering feat of such great originality, and an innovation in architecture so complete, that the effects must have survived somewhere in the following years. But such we cannot find. Roofed buildings of so great an expanse do not come for centuries.

(2) *Practical Possibility.* If we are historically justified in daring to doubt the roofed character of Solomon's Temple, we are likewise justified in acknowledging the practical difficulty of roofing such a space.

Solomon's Temple was twenty cubits broad and sixty-odd long, inside measure (i. e., not counting the surrounding stories of chambers). A cubit seems to have corresponded to an Egyptian ell, which was about 20⅔ inches. The building cubit apparently was

a handbreadth longer than the cubit in ordinary use.[34] This ne-
cessitates a roof that shall clear a little over thirty-four feet, the
shortest way for the timbers. Could cedar beams support a roof
of planks and stamped earth of such dimensions, when the longitudinal sagging would still more increase the weight? On the
face of it, it is absurd.[35] Some other shift must be devised to meet
the demand. Stade[36] suggests some kind of trusses springing from
the upper walls on both sides, but this is both ungraceful and un-
supported by historic precedent or Biblical data (though the latter
lack is not overmuch to be considered). Even so the weight would
be most uncomfortably great, and no competent means of fastening
such braces to the wall is thinkable for the period considered. It
has been suggested that the ceiling beams may have been warped
before they were put in place, to counteract by the upthrust of their
artificial curve the downthrust of the roof. Disregarding the historical possibility of such knowledge, there are still two other facts
that make such a thing doubtworthy: (a) a warped beam under
pressure will not stay warped forever, especially if moisture can get
at it (as moisture eventually could through stamped earth), and
(b) there would be a lateral thrust exerted upon the walls which
would be considerable from such weight, if the warping carried
the center of the beam anything above the level of insertion. These
walls were thick, but were put together without cohesive cement
of any kind.

A still further possibility is that of Schmidt[37] who suggests
columns five cubits from each side wall to form a support for the
rest of the wall (making a clerestory), basing his suggestion on
1 Kings x. 12. Aside from the unreliability of the verse, such a
possibility is unthinkable. Clerestories were first heard of in Ro-
manesque and Gothic architecture. Also think of the weight the
"almug tree" supports would have to carry; the roof weight (though
narrowed, still appreciable) and all but ten cubits of the side walls,
i. e., twenty vertical cubits of stone! To say nothing of the difficulties
this would get us into with the peripheral chambers!

Fergusson[38] argues for eight pillars in the Holy Place, sup-

[34] Deuteronomy iii, (אַמָּה אִישׁ) as compared with Ezekiel xl. 5 and xliii.
13, and 2 Chron. iii. 3.

[35] Strabo (Bk. XIV, C I, Casabeb 634) says: "The Milesians built a temple
which exceeded in size all others, but it remained without a roof on account
of its size." This is much later. If we only knew the dimensions!

[36] Siegfried Stade, ZATW, iii, ad. loc.

[37] Cf. Commentary on Kings ad loc.

[38] Fergusson. The Temples of the Jews, p. 28 f.

porting the roof nearer its center. This is most reasonable of all. But the difficulty of forty-five or fifty-foot pillars made of wood is obvious, as is also the necessity of some lateral tie, part of the distance up. I Kings x. 12 and I Kings xviii. 6 are cited as his justification, and also the existence of the ten lamps etc. as arguing ten spaces to be filled.[39]

But all these difficulties are overcome in the idea of a court, open to the sky, with a peristyle surrounding it; which takes in all the pillars necessary, which can very easily contain all the cedar beams and planks mentioned in the "cieling"[40] and which, besides, has the merit of historic lineage.

Such a reconstruction, however, is open to two substantial objections, which must be faced. In the first place we are expressly told in all the accounts that the temple was sheathed within with cedar so that not a stone was to be seen. It would be difficult to keep sheathing in good repair above the line of the peristyle, and it would look queer to see wood on the inside and stone on the outside. I have only two possible suggestions to make. (a) May not "within" mean within the peristyle, i. e., under its cover, where also only the floor would be laid, and no stone seen? (b) May not the "within and without"[41] ascribed to the gold floor covering be analogy enough to prove a like obvious tampering with the text allotting to the carving of the cherubim, palm trees, etc. a similar position?[42]

The second difficulty is the crucial one. Cyprus has no rainy season of any considerable violence or duration. Neither has Egypt. In Palestine, however, more rain falls in three months than the average rainfall of the whole year round in England. An open-court temple would be a dismal and sloppy place during the rainy season. The table of the shewbread etc. could be moved back under the cover of the peristyle, but further protection is necessary. This protection awnings would provide, awnings either of skins or of Tyrian stuff, which was often so thick as surely to be water-proof. Figures 4 and 5 above may evidence the validity of a conjecture also suggested by the common use of awnings in Egypt and Assyria.

So far as the rainy season goes, Phœnicia proper, too, gets its share of rainfall; and the Phœnician style of architecture starts, not

---

[39] I do not consider as worth consideration any such anachronous conjectures as a gable-roof implies. Such a roof cannot have appeared before the time of Herod, at least, i. e., until Greek influence gave the example. Semitic roofs are flat.

[40] I Kings vi. 15-18, etc.

[41] I Kings vi. 30.

[42] I Kings vi. 29.

in Cyprus, but at home. If Phœnicia itself had possessed any rain-proof structure, we probably should have found some evidence of it in her colonies. She would not have been able to keep one style for "home consumption" and another for her "colonial export trade." If the Temple at Jerusalem is faced by the problem of the rainy season, so are the neighboring ones in Tyre and Sidon, whose open courts seem well authenticated.[48]

(3) *Biblical Possibility.* There is evidence of pillars of some kind within the house, as they are repeatedly mentioned. There seem to have been four in the Holy of Holies, but they are not the only ones in the "House" by any means.

As to the ceiling, the Hebrew text need give no data for more than that of a peristyle if there is no preconceived notion to be gotten out of the text. 1 Kings vi. 9 ("he covered the house with beams and boards of cedar") is taken by the Septuagint and a small modern minority to mean the covering of the walls, and 1 Kings vii. 7 certainly shows the same verb can be so used for wainscoting. 1 Kings vi. 15 has the word ceiling in it [44], but it can apply equally well to the ceiling of the peristyle. The beams must have been covered above with limestone as protection from the weather, wherever placed.

I find no decisive reason for abandoning the conclusion to which the architectural pedigree of Solomon's Temple brought me, that it had an open peristylar court. Heredity seems to hold true.

[48] Cf. Biblos, Fig. 6.

[44] Instead of "walls" we must read "beams"—making it "From the floor of the house unto the beams of the ceiling"—which helps the contention above that the sheathing extended only "within" the colonnade.

THE TEMPLE BUILDING.

I. GENERAL DIMENSIONS.

IT is a curious fact that there are but few variations in the ground-plan of the Temple (Fig. 10), since all the data are so comparatively devoted to length and breadth, and not to elevation. The Kings and Chronicles accounts give us the length of the "House" (i. e., of the Temple proper, exclusive of the porch and the surrounding tiers of rooms, which are spoken of continually in a very *removed* way) as sixty cubits in all;[45] forty in the Holy Place (the *Hekal*) and twenty in the Holy of Holies (the *Debir*).[46] These are apparently inside measurements, with no allowance made for the thickness of the dividing partition. Twenty cubits is given as the breadth of both Hekal and Debir.[47] Ezekiel gives the length of the Temple, on the other hand, as one hundred cubits[48] (east to west) and from his account we get our data to fill in the *plan*. The Holy of Holies is twenty cubits, the court is forty, and the porch ten.[49] The rooms back of the Debir are five cubits wide.[50] This gives for room space seventy-five cubits. The chamber-wall at the back is given as five cubits,[51] the "wall of the House" is six cubits,[52] which is both back and front of the "House," the porch door jamb is six cubits likewise,[53] and the dividing wall between the Debir and Hekal fills in the remaining two. This foots up the necessary hundred. The same elements give us the width of the building as fifty-two cubits. The height throughout is given as thirty cubits.[54] On the

[45] 1 Kings vi. 2b.
[46] 2 Chron. iii. 8.
[47] 1 Kings vi. 2b.
[48] Ezek. xli. 15
[49] 1 Kings vi. 3; 2 Chron. iii. 4.
[50] 1 Kings vi. 6. Ezek. xli seems to be wrong (four cubits).
[51] Ezek. xli. 9.
[52] Ezek. xli. 5.
[53] Ezek. xl. 48 plus the extra cubit of the breadth of the porch he gives.
[54] 1 Kings vi. 2.

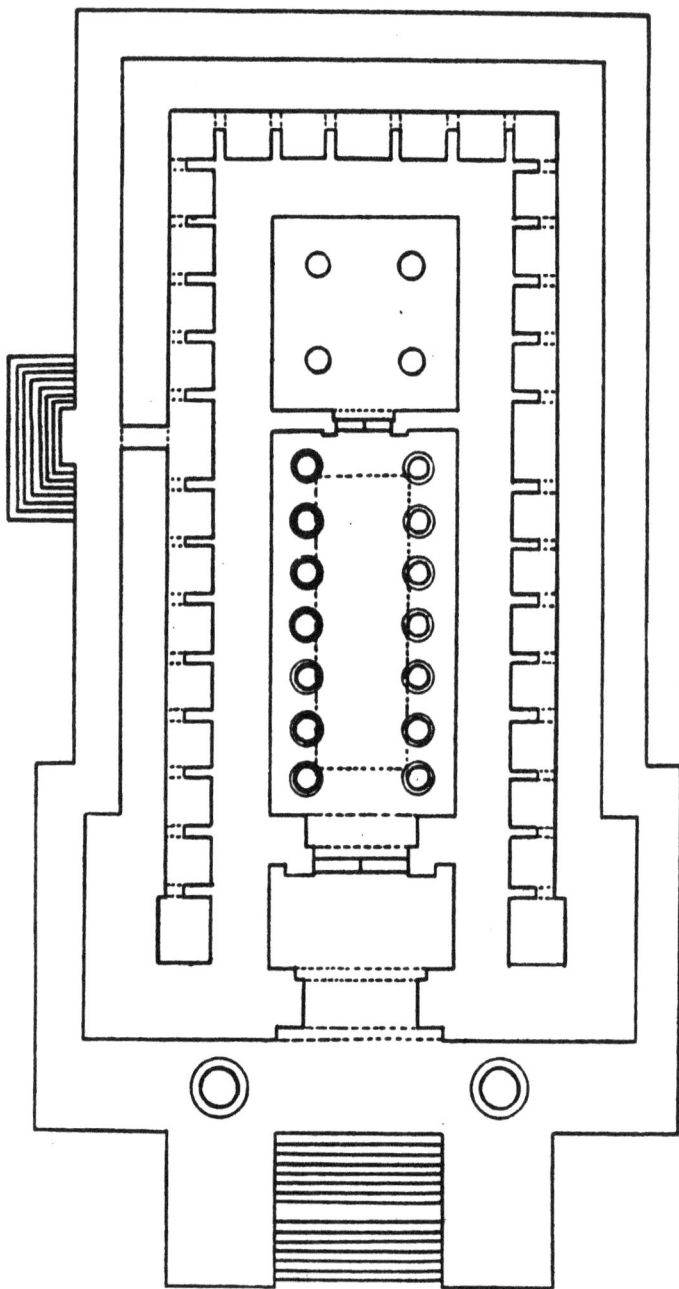

Fig. 10. GROUND PLAN OF TEMPLE.

old and accepted idea of a roofed building, discussion centered much, therefore, on the question whether there was a room over the Holy of Holies, whose cubical form[55] would leave ten cubits' space below the roof, or whether the Debir was externally lower than the roof of the house, or even whether there might not be an upper room over *all* the house.[56] This problem disappears with the open-court idea, leaving the Debir as the only roofed room set in the end of a rectangular space, enclosed by a thirty-cubit wall.

For these and the following details cf. the plan (Fig. 10) and the longitudinal, vertical section (Fig. 11) which better visualize them.

II. THE PORCH.

Upon the front of the Temple building itself rose the porch, though it is always spoken of almost as though it were not joined to the House. Its dimensions are variously given. Twenty cubits seems to have been the width[57] corresponding to the breadth of the House. This, of course is interior measure. The depth (again interior) is given in Kings as ten cubits,[58] but by Ezekiel as eleven.[59] Ten is, of course, the correct number, since Semitic love of proportion would make the porch half the Debir's length, which in its turn was half that of the Hekal. Ezekiel's accuracy, however, I do not doubt; but suggest the usual Egyptian section of the door-jamb which gives the actual door-post a buttress of a few inches; in this case probably a round cubit. This gives the door-jamb a thickness of five cubits, but the wall one of six (cf. plan, Fig. 11).

The height of the porch is not told us except in Chronicles,[60] where it is put at 120 cubits! This is not believable, (though Perrot & Chipiez, recognizing Ezekiel's temple as ideal, give this height as a good climax to the successive gateways.)[61] This of course would be external measure. We have noticed the Chronicler's propensity to exaggeration, which generally takes the form of doubling and quadrupling. Here one-half the given height would be most fitting, giving 60 cubits, which is approximately the length of the house.

---

[55] 1 Kings vi. 20.
[56] Basing the question on the meaning of הָעֲלִיּוֹת (Septuagint τὸ ὑπερῷον) in 2 Chronicles iii. 9, which more obviously means the upper surrounding chambers.
[57] 1 Kings vi. 3. 2 Chron. iii. 4.
[58] 1 Kings vi. 3.
[59] Ezek. xl. 49.
[60] 2 Chron. iii. 4.
[61] Perrot & Chipiez, *Hist. of Art in Sardinia, Judea, Syria and Asia Minor,* Chap. IV, pp. 201 ff.

Fig. 11. SOLOMON'S TEMPLE. LONGITUDINAL SECTION.

This is meagre data but there is possible reinforcement to be found in two other places. Ezra[62] and Esdras[63] inferentially state the propylon to have been 60×60 cubits. These dimensions were in the rescript of Cyrus, which the Jews seem to have brought with them on their return from exile. It is most improbable, when permission to rebuild was given and measurements were specified, that these dimensions should not correspond to the old Temple. When Jerusalem was captured, the Assyrians quite probably noted the details of the Temple as being the most sacred possession of the Jews, and so these records were put in the record-chamber at Babylon or Ecbatana, where Cyrus unearthed them.

But, even accepting these dimensions, the form of the porch is still vague and indeterminate. Conjecture is legitimate. Some modification of the Egyptian pylon[64] is most naturally to be supplied. As we look at the Paphos coins we see a rudimentary pylon facing us. The flanking masses, as compared with the Egyptian originals, are shrunken in width almost to the appearance of pillars. The doorway, in proportion, has enlarged. How shall we interpret these "pictures"? In the first place, the narrowing of the pylons may be arbitrary, to show the side wings, which in reality are behind them, just as the "ashera pillars" are in reality in front of them. The raising of the doorway may be for the sake of giving the representation of the sacred cone more room. The coins give us an abstraction of an architectural form which in itself was likewise an abstraction of Egyptian forms. The gateway, it is clear, was to the Phœnician the most impressive adjunct of the temple; and the mention of the porch in all three Biblical accounts with such emphasis gives a slight degree of probability to the same deduction in Jerusalem, which is further increased by reassertion of Phœnician authorship. If this is true, Egypt need not supply all the material for reconstruction. Assyria may largely be drawn upon for ornamentation and subsidiary forms.

I do not believe the gateway of the Temple to have been a single (sloping-sided) plinth, as some reconstructions have suggested. The three parts to a gateway of any importance are to be found both in Egypt, Phœnicia and Assyria, (though in the last the sloping walls are absent). A doorway, flanked by buttress-masses rising above its crown on either side, seems obvious. Whether the doorway was recessed or salient between them is debatable, but

[62] Ezra vi. 1 ff.
[63] 1 Esdras vi. 22 ff.
[64] Cf. Fig. 6, p. 626.

I have chosen the recessed doorway (as against Egyptian precedent) because the Paphos coins seem slightly to favor such a de-

Fig. 12. ASSYRIAN GATEWAY.
Southeastern gateway of Sargon's Palace at Khorsabad. (Com-
piled from Thomas by Perrot & Chipiez, *Chaldea and Assyria,*
Vol. II, p. 17, pl. 5.)

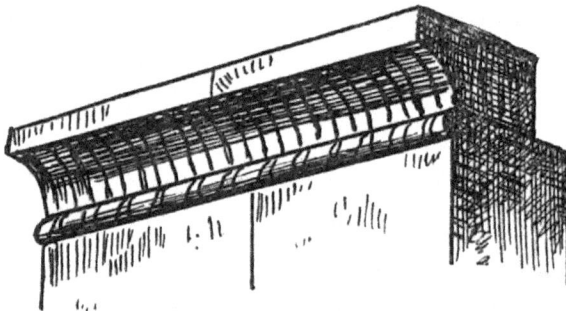

Fig. 13. THE EGYPTIAN GORGE OR CORNICE.
Perrot & Chipiez, *Egypt,* Vol. I, p. 102, fig. 67.

cision, and because in Ezekiel's measurements of the porch we are
told that the breadth of the door(gate) was "three cubits on this

side and three cubits on that"[65] which I take to mean the breadth
of the doorposts on their outside face, showing some kind of demarcation from the surface beyond. This is well within the realm
of probability, especially since it follows the Assyrian type of gateway (Fig. 12) to some degree, and we know the Phœnicians used
the Assyrian stepped ornament wherever they found a possible
chance.

The predominant effect, however, must have been more Egyptian than Assyrian, since the sloping lines of the buttresses are the
dominant features. I have crowned the buttresses and the doorway

Fig. 14. SOLOMON'S TEMPLE. FRONT ELEVATION.

with the Egyptian gorge (Fig. 13), in turn surmounted by the
Assyrian stepped ornament, a favorite Phœnician trick.

The doorway may have been almost any height. Many have put
Jachin and Boaz under its architrave as supporting pillars, making
its height equal to their twenty-three cubits. But in my idea of the
Temple, Jachin and Boaz are most assuredly the porch (cf. § XIV
below). The portal must be impressive, but its inner wall cannot
go above the insert of the roof of the peristyle within, if that is to
surround the Hekal on all four sides. I have therefore made the
outer opening twenty-three cubits high, and the inner one, in which
were placed the great doors of olive wood, comes down to twelve.

[a] Ezekiel xl. 45.

The porch as viewed from the front (east) is shown in the elevation given in Fig. 14.

III. THE HEKAL.

There is but little that need be said about the Hekal when it is once decided what its fate shall be. The only questions to be settled are the height of the peristyle and the crowning wall, if any, above the Debir. I have set the height of the peristyle at twelve cubits, above which the facing carries the apparent height another three. I have made the colonnade of a single row of pillars which carry the architrave five cubits out from the wall (i. e., counting from the base. The slant of the walls would add about half a cubit at the indicated height).[46] Since the pillars were of wood I have used the simplest form of wooden pillar Egypt knew, as more easily sheathed in case such sheathing should be necessary to suppose. The windows which are several times mentioned in the description of the "House" I take to be those of the peripheral rooms and merely for the sake of ventilation; and these would probably pierce the wall of the house only at a place where they would not be visible from the floor; i. e., only those of the top tier of rooms can have been let into the Hekal, which would come so low down above the peristyle roof and behind its facing that they would be totally hidden from below. These were probably latticed and smaller at the outside than within the rooms. The Debir, being ten cubits below the cornice of the House-wall, would look queer unless its front edge were marked somehow. This is easily done by a rather tall cornice, surmounted by the useful and ubiquitous stepped ornament, whose top level easily would reach the base of the House-wall's gorge.

IV. THE DEBIR.

As has already been said, the Debir was a cube of twenty cubits inside measurement. It was absolutely dark, there being no windows opening into it. "Yahveh loveth darkness" seems to have been a common conception of the time.[47] There is some doubt, nevertheless, of the doors being kept closed. The staves of the Ark seem to have been visible from the outer Hekal.[48] These doors

---

[46] Does not this slant of the walls explain that phrase of Ezekiel's which has given such trouble: "The breadth of the house was still upward"? Ezekiel xli. 7b.

[47] I Kings viii. 12; 2 Chron. vi. 1.

[48] I Kings viii. 8. The verse is not altogether clear but seems to warrant this much.

folded vertically.[69] The doorway appears to have been pentagonal,[70] an additional distinction, marking the dignity of the entrance. It was six cubits broad.[71] The height is not given; probably it would come to about ten cubits. The four necessary posts of the sanctuary would be about five cubits from the walls, in order to have the central space clear for the Ark and its guarding cherubim.

V. THE CHAMBERS.

The chambers are a fairly unique phenomenon; yet their presence cannot be doubted, because of the unusual and accurate agreement of the accounts. Also such chambers have been discovered at Birs Nimrud (Egypt),[72] and the British Museum Gem (Fig. 5), though later, shows that the Phœnicians knew how to combine such a feature with their temple-type.

The chambers were in three stories, extending on all sides of the "House" except the east, where the porch took up all the space.

The method of their superposition is most ingenious, yet simple. Owing to the veneration for the "House" it was deemed sacrilegious to insert timbers in its walls. So rebatements of one cubit per story gave resting-ledges for the cedar(?) timbers upon which the floors were laid. This of course necessitated an enlarging of the rooms; so that, the rooms on the first story being five cubits wide, the second story rooms were six and the top one seven. The height of all seems to have been the same, i. e., five cubits.[73] Their outer wall, according to Ezekiel was five cubits thick. Whether the rebatement was shared by both House and chamber wall is uncertain, but from the repeated statement of the narrowed rests in the "wall of the House" and the lack of a single word about a like lessening in the chamber-wall, it seems likeliest that the whole rebatement of one cubit a story took place in the "House" wall. The exterior slant of the wall of the chambers keeps parallel to the successive lessening of the main wall, which continued to slant inward above the top chamber.

Connection was made from one room to another without the mediacy of a corridor. I have placed the doors next the outer wall, as being simpler to construct and as providing more storage space in the rooms. There was a door-way in the bottom tier of rooms on the south side of the building. Ezekiel's addition of one on the

[69] The veil which Chronicles describes is later. Neither Ezekiel nor Kings mention it.
[70] I Kings vi. 31b = "five-square."
[71] Ezekiel xli. 3.
[72] cf. Fergusson, *Hist. of Architecture*, ad loc.
[73] I Kings vi. 10.

north seems to be a gratuitous personal gift to the ideal he had. Although there were winding stairways in Egyptian pylons, it is doubtful if such skill was yet attained elsewhere. Ladders are a more imaginable means of ascent, though stairs may have been built in by the time of the exile. To put these ladders only on the south side at the doorway room is to leave communication highly difficult. Therefore, as is the natural historical impulse, I have run the rooms well into the buttress-masses of the pylon (which *must* have been built partially hollow) and provided a doorway opening out across the porch's roof. Probably ladders were also to be found in these pylon rooms, which may possibly have been larger by a little than the others.

The number of these rooms is doubtful. Ezekiel is the only one who mentions their number, and he does it in such a way as to defy the best Chinese puzzle-solver. Whether there were thirty in all, thirty-three in all, thirty in each story or thirty-three in each story is an apparently insoluble question. I have chosen thirty-three to a story as working out the best in my plan, but there is no guide to such a choice except convenience.[74]

The windows of these rooms were also latticed, to keep out birds, rain, etc. There must have been a slight slant to the roof of the top story and a perforation through the outer wall to let rain run off. Probably the roof of the Debir drained backward likewise onto the chamber-roof, through small spouts in the "House"-wall.

VI. MATERIAL.

Jerusalem and its vicinity is well provided with excellent building stone, the *maleki,* a hard style of chalk or white, hard limestone, still appreciated at the present day. It can be polished like marble. It was cut in the quarry to the desired shape and size and brought to its place in the temple, so that no sound of iron was heard in the whole process of building.[75] Doubtless this was in deference to a popular superstition which forbade the use of iron on any sacred house, as shown in the oldest legislation of the Hebrews by the prohibition of altars of *hewn* stone, because the lifting of a tool upon it would defile it.[76]

---

[74] To be sure, this makes pretty small rooms, but they were for storage-closets etc., not for living-rooms. Storage-closets need not have been large, since all the priestly paraphernalia and treasures seem to have been portably small.

[75] Although the authenticity of the verse (1 Kings vi. 7) has been doubted owing to its queer position, historic likelihood renews the idea.

[76] Ex. xx. 25:

Timber was and is of inferior quality and meagre quantity. Hence a treaty with Hiram was necessary to obtain sufficient cedar and cypress for the prodigal sheathing and colonnades (in the courtyards and Solomon's palaces especially) the plans called for. The forests of Lebanon and of Cyprus are evidenced even now. Hiram had his timber next door.

The gold seems to have been later imagination. But gilding and charging with bronze (brass) is a characteristic Phœnician trick and we need not leave this out of the ornamental possibilities of the Temple.

This finishes the bare reconstruction of the building Solomon dedicated to Yahveh as the permanent abiding-place of His Ark. Yet the ornamentation and symbolic or semi-symbolic details contain so much more of the live interest of the times that, at the great risk of tediousness, I must say a few words on three of the more noticeable birth-marks of the Temple: (1) Jachin and Boaz, (2) the sacred trees, and (3) the Cherubim.

DECORATIVE AND SYMBOLICAL DETAILS.

IF it is natural to approach the work of reconstructing the Temple in a tentative spirit, it is many times more natural so to approach the more widely and diversely evidenced and much discussed symbolism of the Temple's details, especially the twin pillars that stood in the porch of the Temple, Jachin and Boaz; for the question of their form is bound up firmly with that of their significance and is largely dependent upon it. The interest of the Temple, too, must be more in such live evidences of ancient thought and culture than in the reshaping of hard stones, whose cold outlines, even when blended into the organic unity of the building, must be more or less the end-in-itself, rather than the interpretive means to an understanding of the humanity which made it. Details are more illuminative than architectural entireties, for the very reason that they best can express concrete thoughts and moods.

In the beginning of this thesis I found it convenient to presuppose the necessity of two axioms, claiming them to be constructive data for my argument. The former of them was this, that *Judaism embodies a religious genius as yet not unique.* I must claim its aid once more at the crux of this present puzzle, repeating that "in spite of the superiority over neighboring faiths which comes to the worship of Yahveh from its dawning henotheistic monotheism, *there are common elements still retained, proclaiming blood relationship with the rest of the Semitic world, however polytheistic it may be.*" It is hard not to believe that in the Temple we find the symbols of the earlier stages of Yahvism, which are also kindred to contemporary worship—symbols of neighboring and kindred nations.

II.

Perhaps the commonest element of all old-world religions is the reverence for the pillar. It is surprising to see how few things there are of which Egypt is not the ultimate parent, whether it is motives employed in art, or religious ideas and representations. Of course, Mesopotamian civilization succeeded in stamping as individually its own much that is apparently the outcome of its peculiar culture; but we are now able to see very numerous details and elementary ideals which go back of old Assyrian and old Babylonian into still older Egypt; whose travels to the Tigris and Euphrates, just as also to Asia Minor and the Greek islands and Greece itself are rendered intelligible only by the mediacy of Phœnician ships. This is especially true of tree worship, which is the concomitant of *betylae*, or pillar worship.

When motives of religious art pass from one people to another, the myth sometimes accompanies the type on its migrations, but oftener it lags behind; the religious symbol is first naturalized and its mythological significance follows later. Or perhaps the symbol alone is adopted; the meaning it held in its native climate being far different from the meaning it is christened with, if new meaning there is at all, in its adoptive home. We cannot deduce from the contemporary appearance of a symbol in diverse nations that it necessarily means the same in each. Unless evidences of similar myths and ideals are to be found, the symbol's presence stands for little. But in the earlier days of Yahveh-worship these similar modes of worshiping similar symbols are obviously present, so that Phœnician religion may be fairly used as the data for the possible ground-work of Hebrew faith, however higher than the foundation its later evolution may build.

Throughout the earlier Old Testament we continually run across the worship of Ashera. The circumstances, however, connote no very clear identification with anything we know. Is Ashera a deity, sometimes given "human" form? Is Ashera an embodiment of Astarte-Ashtoreth? Or is Ashera the symbolization of the nature-mother in tree-form? As a symbol, attribute or utensil of worship the Ashera seems to meet us only in the cultus of feminine deities. In its most original form, as archeology has mapped its stages out,[77] we have a single object, the emblem of this feminine deity, soon appearing in the company of her male correlative. These two

---

[77] Cf. Max Ohnefalsch-Richter, *Kypros, the Bible and Homer.* Text; from which I have most of my data on this subject.

symbols may be two similar or dissimilar trees, posts, pillars or cones. At any rate the agalmata are so far aniconic. These two symbols either manifest the presence and joint rule of a godling and little goddess in a holy place, or they show that a single deity is thought of as a double nature (i. e., androgynous, both male and female at once).

To these rude symbols soon are added heads, extremities and other anthropomorphic details, until at last they become true images.[78] Interruptions and reversions halt and hinder the process thus slightly sketched, but the evolutionary trend is clear.

When this final stage is reached that god who attained anthropomorphic form is regarded as dwelling in the more primitive types, in the tree, in the cone, or the post, and may be represented under those forms; or the tree, post or cone becomes the main idol of the non-idol-confined god, the convenient object of offerings and sacrifices.[79]

The constant descriptions of the Asherim in the Bible, especially when they occur in conjunction with mention of the altars of Baal and Masseboth[80] leaves little doubt that beside the Baal-pillar, the Masseba or Chamman, we must recognize the presence of the Ashera-tree or wooden Ashera-post[81] (frequently burned as sacrifice), representing the *paredros* any localized god may have, just as he may have a representation of Ashtoreth.[82] Baal is simply the word for "god." —Yahveh is as yet a Baal.[83] The tree-goddess Ashera is only another form of Ashtoreth-Astarte, who herself is often symbolized in tree form. The Ashera is nothing but a local Ashtoreth or Baal-consort, who has preserved in a purer form and for a longer period her primitive and pristine character of a tree or wooden post, "the vegetative ground-work of her nature." The lunar side of Astarte (connected with the solar worship of her mate) is peculiar to the general and ideal goddess, not to her local abodes or Ashera symbols.

Under Phœnician influence all the Canaanitic and Cyprian god-

[78] Cf. Fig. 26 where the sacred tree shows clear signs of embryonic humanity—which anthropomorphism is clarified in the two tracings at the top.

[79] Aerolites never outgrew this heaven-sent character (super-aniconic).

[80] E. g., Exodus xxxiv. 13.

[81] It is interesting to note, that, although as a rule monuments are silent witnesses, with one or two exceptions only, all the pillar-monuments we have from the region of Phœnician influence mention somewhere on them the name "Ashera."

[82] Judges ii. 13; iii. 7; 1 Kings xviii and xix.

[83] Cf. many Pentateuchal names written without distinction with the ending Baal or Bosheth (Yahveh), e. g., Ishbaal = Ishbosheth and Mephibaal = Mephibosheth and also the meaningful name Baaliah (Baal = Jah).

desses are derived from the single primitive feminine deity found most clearly in primitive Babylonia, from whom anthropomorphic form evolves most variously. Similarly when these same Canaanites and Cyprians reached the stage where they substituted an anthropomorphic *god* for the pillar-representative of the male deity, it was Bel-Baal, husband of Belit-Balat (Mylitta) who was the model. They are the pattern Lord and Lady from which local shrines adapt their patron deities.

III.

This is many years before the Temple of Solomon, although even then contemporary development outside of Israel was little above this stage. The simple Baal-Ashera symbols had developed into a particularization of attributes little found in Judea. From this simple scaffold-faith there had elsewhere set in a specialization in three directions.

 a. Sex-symbols became no longer subsidiary to mere purposes of identification, but symbols in themselves of great sig·· nificance.

 b. Sacred trees became more and more definite in botanical separation.

 c. The sun and moon became identified with the divine duality.

We find the demarcation of these three tendencies already begun in the time of the later Pentateuch. Kings shows evidences of the resultant conditions, if we look between the lines.

 a. The Ashera began to be surmounted by sex-signets. As made of wood, the feminine, vegetative, symbol of the post became more the localized incarnation of nature, the vegetative All-mother The stone pillar of a Baal became the symbol of its transcending god's masculinity. The phallus was first mounted upon it; then the pillar itself assumed the phallic character. The feminine symbol, the triangle, at first upon the apex of the Ashera-post, became the cone of the goddess, the outline of which was that same triangle. Thus grew up the phallic specialization and interpretation of the life of the universe which we of to-day find so hard to comprehend sympathetically.

The Semite cast all his gods more or less in one mold; the Greek specialized and articulated his, never allowing them to overlap functions in the divine economy of the universe. All Semitic pantheons are therefore permeated with a solution of phallicism, as well as with the solutions of other tendencies, until they seem all of a piece. We find little differentiation between vegetative and sexual attributes, since vegetative ideas and sexual ideas have affected all the gods so much that they are no longer distinguished from each other, nor in their individual make-up is the same mapping-out and separation possible. It required a long time for mankind to reach that stage where abstract ideals could be formulated and acted upon. The individual, concrete, kindergarten celebration of some visible, suggestive symbol-ritual was the only means of spiritual approach to disembodied life. But a single act of ritual would be explicable in all sorts of ways, the varying interpretations, vegetative, sexual, etc., blending into homogeneity through the medium of the visible, concrete act, although heterogeneous except for this thought-producing, variously-explicable symbol, their point in common.

If, then, the sexual idea permeated the conception of one god, his *paredros* would straightway catch the same infection. The Baal, conceived as the husband of the land he fertilized,[84] made inevitable by his phallic emphasis a like metamorphosis of his goddess-wife. He did not specialize into an individual with the definite attribute of sexual fertility and let his goddess go her vegetative way, but he gave to her his characteristic flavor and soaked himself in hers, so that they held a community of qualities, rather than becoming private quality-estate owners. The sexual tendency develops not as individualized in any deity, but as a separable, yet never separated, element in the evolution of the whole spiritual compound. It is nevertheless a specialization from the primitive Baal-pillar and its genetic content.

b. The second specialization descends from the Ashera-post side of the family. Although the principle of fertility is one and indivisible, this vegetative tendency is indubitably distinguishable. Tree worship took its suffragette equality in the worship of the fruitful principles of the universe. The all-mother character could be vegetatively explained as validly as in sexual terms. The pomegranate was sacred to the first all-mother; as being with its great productive powers an appropriate signum of her essence. Hence, too, we find the pomegranate sacred everywhere to the goddess who occupies the seat of Ashtoreth in the native pantheon. In Cyprus it was Aphrodite herself who planted it:[85] it was sacred to Adonis (Tammuz) her partner,[86] and was bound up in the theo-

---

[84] Cf. Asshur of the Assyrian Trinity.

[85] Cf. Antiphanes quoted by Athenæus, III, p. 84c.

[86] "In the Temenos of Aphrodite at Dali was found a model of a pomegranate in terra cotta (natural size) and many of the crouching figures of the

genetic myths of Phrygia.[57] The pomegranate is sacred in Egypt to the "Warmhearted" Isis. It seems to be of Semitic origin; Homer mentions it only once. Even to-day the people of Cyprus use its countless seeds as a symbol of fertility. The Assyrians gave another tree sacred prominence, the palm. Conventional and far removed from life as their sculptured palmettes may seem, only palm withes could be so plaited; and the leaves are unmistakable. The elements of the Mesopotamian sacred tree are to be found in Egypt and all the ports to which Phœnician influence extended.

This worship of sacred trees we find in the Old Testament in the "groves" at which the iconoclastic anger of the reformers so arose, but it was the deeds perpetrated in their shadow that were the downfall of the heretical high places (*bamoth*), not the sacredness of the trees, which were found even in Solomon's own Temple ornamentation. The sacred tree worship was too closely tied to the glorification of the reproductive powers of the universe to escape the stigma of the latter's excesses. But those who find in the representations of the sacred tree merely a frank feminine signum go too far in their preconceived programme of reducing all cultus symbols to sexuality.

These two specializations, sexual and vegetative, exist side by side in the same symbols and rituals. When the king, personating some Baal, married some Ashera image or some Temple-prostitute, personating in her turn the goddess whose priestess she was, it was both a recognition of the sexuality of the workings of the universe and a ritual of "homoeopathic magic"[58] whereby the fertility of the land, the revival of the trees and the increase of all nature, was insured. (It is a familiar tenet of all magic that the imitation of a desired result procures it). Thus, for instance, the early Phœnician kings of Paphos or their sons claimed to be not merely the priests of the goddess but her semi-divine lovers, personating Adonis. The original myth of Pygmalion and the image was in all probability some such manifested Astarte-wedding.

c. Sun- and moon-worship is a third interpretation of the life of the divine pair, merging with phallicism and nature-worship. The

youthful Adonis (votive) hold in their hands—among other fruits— the pomegranate." Ohnefalsch-Richter, *Kypros, the Bible and Homer* (Text).

[58] Adonis = Lord. "The name does not signify Tammuz in the Bible unless so specified. But the cult was rampant (cf. Ezekiel). For an innocent usage, cf. also the names Adoni-kam (Ezra ii. 13), Adoni-ram (1 Kings, iv. 6), Adoni-jah (1 Kings i. 15).

[58] Adonis, Attis, Osiris, Frazer, pp. 14 and 30.

sun as the productive energy in the world[*] was worshiped in Phœnicia in this fashion, not in the later abstract form of Persian Zoroastrianism. Sun and moon are merely another manifestation of the *genos* and *genea* of all life (although the *lunar* aspect is also necessarily more or less identified with a *nature*-goddess).

All these three specializations existed in advanced forms, had their specialized cults and rituals as quasi-sectarian bodies. Yet the primitive pillar-pair still contained the essential germs of all three specializations and had its more comprehensive, if less intensive, meaning and appeal.

Jachin and Boaz stood in the porch of Solomon's temple. Their workmanship was such that they seem to have been the most famous incident of the whole construction. Bronze-casting was very obviously unfamiliar to the Jews. But it is hard to believe that mere artisan perfection gave them all their fame,—there must have been some symbolism implied that redounded to the glory of Yahveh. This significance I find in their being a sign of the androgynous nature of Yahveh. While the more primitive intensity of quality-personification may somewhat have dwindled away, let us remind ourselves that orthodox high places were still in open and general use; that Baalim and Ashera-Teraphim existed without question at high-places of neighboring, kindred gods; that we are halfway between the golden calf in the wilderness and the destruction of calf-worship in the northern kingdom, which had been instituted to counteract the lack of Jerusalemitic worship by symbolizing the attributes of Yahveh; that Jachin and Boaz themselves bore facsimiles of pomegranates.

I do not find any definite phallic symbolism in them, nor any specialized tree-signification. They represent to me the continuance of the unspecialized betylae-pair, holding in their solution the male and female elements, nature and phallic-cult basic ideas, patron and patroness protectorate, and the solar and lunar manifestations of their qualities. Precipitation and separation of these half-identical attributes into concrete symbolism has not here taken place, as elsewhere. The Temple remains aniconic, and therefore all-inclusive of possible significance. The devout believer in Yahveh may claim for him any attribute he feels to be inherent in the deity he wants to worship, and point to Jachin and Boaz as the sign-manual of his right to do so. It is perfectly possible that they may signify anything evolved from that type in whose form they anachronously

---

[*] הֵילֵל = the Impregnator.

survive and defy the specialization whose seeds have otherwhere
flowered and fruited into special ritual, special emblems, special
cult-sects. Indeed, it is perfectly possible that the setting-up of a
betylae-pair before the Temple, from the very fact that it was the
primitive seed of the too obviously flowering specializations round
about, was the very thing to call the attention of the worshiper
back to the really simple and potent essence which was so masked

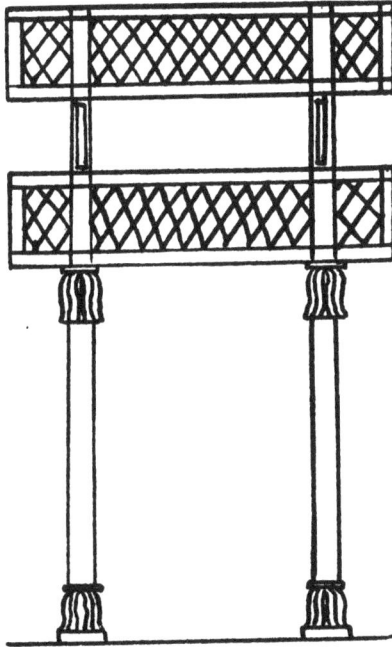

Fig. 15. JACHIN AND BOAZ.
(Fergusson, *The Temples of the Jews*, p. 157, fig. 35.)

by their vagaries and exaggerations. Jachin and Boaz proclaimed
the simple creed of true Yahvism.

IV.

This intensifying of meaning in the two pillars seems to do
away with two forms of reconstruction. Stade makes them stand
within the porch, supporting the architrave of its lintel-structure.
Fergusson conjectures that the two pillars upheld a screen, upon
which abundant space was provided for all the ornamentation heart
could wish. (Fig. 15.)

The change of material does not necessitate a change of func-

tion. Many writers contend that, since sacred pillars heretofore had
been made of wood or of stone, this change into metal argues a
change of significance and of function. I cannot see that this follows. Bronze was the *ne plus ultra* of the up-to-date mode. Furthermore, anything with so much significance and prestige as there
seems to have been here involved would hardly have been put to a
comparatively menial, because utilitarian and structural, use. Any
amount of skill would hardly single out two door-posts for such
fame. They must have been objects in themselves, not in any sense
subsidiary to something else. As such they were outstanding obelisks, I feel sure.

Fergusson's[90] suggestion is likewise vetoed by this same in-
tensification of meaning as sufficient explanation of their honor.
His objection to simple pillars is that they do not provide space
enough for the wealth of ornamentation ascribed to them, "nets
of checkerwork, and wreaths of chain work, lily work" and pomegranates by the hundred.[91] This seems true, but is counterbalanced

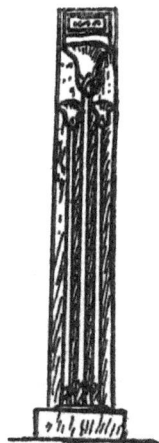

Fig. 16. ORNA-
MENTED PIER
FROM KARNAK.*

Cf. Perrot and Chi-
piez, *Egypt*, II, 94.

by the very evident desire of the author to make
the most of every detail for the glory of Yahveh
himself, whose house is thus, even to minutest details, perfect in its execution. Influenced, however,
by the occurrence of a screen before Herod's
Temple, Fergusson goes to India for analogy and
prototypes. He finds there in the common topes
of Indian temples good opportunity for all the
prodigality of ornament to be desired. But he
knows more about India than Judea, for to go
so far afield brands the search a desperate one,
especially since no connecting link is at present
to be shown.

Why not be content with simple, free-
standing pillars, whose great uniqueness lies in
their material and unexcelled workmanship, but
whose symbolism adds the halo of sanctity to the
sheen of their brass? In Egypt, the stone obelisks stand out *free* before the pylons (Fig. 16
and note); in all the representations of the Pa-
phian temple the flanking pillars or cones are obvious; the pseudo-
Lucian tells of the two great Priapi of Bacchus at the Byblos-

* Fergusson, *The Temples of the Jews*. Text on "Solomon's Temple."
* 1 Kings vii. 17-20.
* This is not the ordinary Egyptian obelisk (cf. "Cleopatra's Needle," Cen-

shrine, into the top of which twice a year a man climbed up, as he would a palm tree, and there abode for seven days. In front of the sanctuary-place of Astarte-Mikal at Kition in Cyprus the remains of columns with Ionizing capitals were found as holy betylae in the customary place. In a small terra-cotta model of a shrine of Venus Urania (as proven by the dove-cote holes) we find a clearer reproduction of one of the later forms these pillars took. (Fig. 17.) Owing to the necessity of support from the fragility of the material of the model the capitals barely touch the wall behind, but this certainly is not the state of things the model intends to portray, since the columns do not support the tiny pent-house above the kennel-like door.

Fig. 17. MODEL OF A SHRINE IN TERRA COTTA.

(Louvre.) Height 8½ in. M. Ohnefalsch-Richter, *Kypros, the Bible and Homer*, pl. CXXXIV. Perrot and Chipiez, *Phœnicia*, p. 287, fig. 208.

The law of parsimony must also rule out the use of Jachin and Boaz as candle-sticks, burning the fat of sacrificed animals; though some of the later temple coins of the Roman era indicate this adaptation. Those of Sardia show the flames. This is a later and utilitarian adaptation of the columns, which would not be thinkable until their emblematic content had been forgotten, which, in the

tral Park, New York, for that) but one of a pair which stand before the pylon of Karnak, whose "saturation" of meaning is greater than any other present example there. Originally these were surmounted by some kind of sacred symbol, perhaps bronze hawks. The bronze has stained the pillars. This gives an example of an Egyptian baetylic'pillar *closely* analogous to Baal and Ashera masseboth in the stage where specialization is just beginning.

time of Solomon was certainly not the case anywhere in the Mediterranean world.

Simplicity is the key-note of their interpretation (cf. figs. 18 and 19) ; not specific specialization of attribute, not mere utilitarian blazonry. In the betylae-character is enough meaning to be worthy of the house of Yahveh. What shall be the definite aspect of the

Fig. 18. PHOENICIAN
MARBLE PILLAR

26 in. high. Louvre. Perrot and Chipiez, *Phœnicia*, Vol. I, p. 131, fig. 72. Ohnefalsch-Richter, *Kypros, the Bible and Homer*, pl. LXXX, fig. 7.

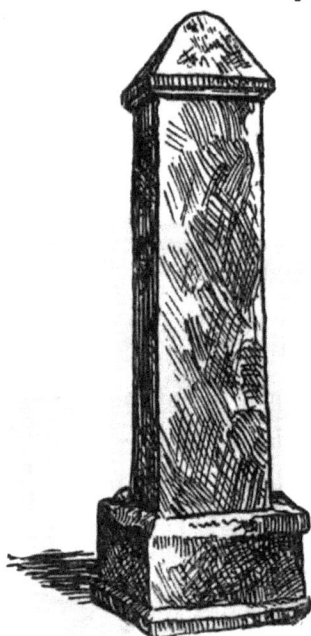

Fig. 19. PHOENICIAN PILLAR.
(Baal Pillar, Phallic.)

Ohnefalsch-Richter, *Kypros, the Bible and Homer*, pl. LXXX. fig. 5.

twin columns? I would not dare to say. The reconstruction given by Perrot and Chipiez meets any demand this line of interpretation can put upon them, as simple symbols of the androgynous, all-comprehending nature of Yahveh, god of Israel.[92]

In the Temple of Solomon as in a museum there were ranged

[92] "It is by no means impossible that the two words [Jachin and Boaz] were within, like talismanic graffiti by the Phœnician founders upon the columns. Let (God it) keep upright by (his) strength" and that in the course of time the two magic words were taken for the names of the columns by persons not very conversant with Phoenician matters." Renan, *Hist. of Israel*, vol. II.

throughout tangible relics of all the stages through which the worship of its God had grown, existing side by side. The exhibit of its most primitive stage is in Jachin and Boaz (divested of the latter-day skill with which the betylae-symbol had been clothed), the common element with all pillar-worship of the Semitic world.

V.

The interior of the Temple showed no single stone, so thoroughly was it sheathed within. We read[93] that Solomon "carved all the walls of the house round about with carved figures of cherubims and palm trees and open flowers, within and without." There

Fig. 20. ASSYRIAN "TREE OF LIFE."
From Layard, *Nineveh.* Plates. Also Perrot and Chipiez, *Chaldea and Assyria.* Vol. I, p. 213.

is grave and most legitimate doubt about the authenticity of all the passages which ascribe the sheathing of so much of the Temple with gold,[94] but this need not rule out the carving of the wooden sheathing, which we would have every historical and archeological reason to expect and suspect if it had not been set forth in our accounts. Egyptian and Assyrian precedent combining in Phœ-

---

[93] I Kings vi. 29; also Ezekiel xli. 18.
[94] Cf. Stade's and Benzinger's commentaries on passages, Stade, ZATW, iii, 140 ff.

nician usage, witnessed to in Mycenaean and Cyprian ruins (though
very meagrely, it is true), seem altogether to give authority to this
hypothesis.

The "palm trees" so repeatedly used must have been some form
of the Assyrian "tree of life" (Fig. 20). And the conventional
design, as I said before, can be only a palm-tree. Even to-day the
peasants of Cyprus plait palm-withes in much the same form.

In Phœnicia the palmette is frequently met; but, true to its
character as a borrowed motive, it is even
more conventional than in Assyria and much
simplified. This trend toward simplification
brings out the residue of Egyptian form the
Assyrian hand so remodeled and disguised (cf.
Fig. 21). The stem has now become an archi-

Fig. 21. ALABASTER SLAB.

Louvre. Height 20 in. From Arados. Cf. Perrot and Chipiez, *Phœnicia and Cyprus*, Vol. I,
p. 134, fig. 76.

Fig. 22. FLORAL PILLAR.

Perrot and Chipiez, *Egypt*,
Vol. II, p. 89, fig. 62.

tectonic column with rudimentary volutes, with four or five rigid
leaves far removed indeed from the vegetable world; even more
de-naturized than its Mesopotamian model. Compare with this the
elaborate Egyptian floral pillar here given (Fig. 22) as just as
possible a prototype and ancestor of the Phœnician palmette as the

Assyrian. Figure 21 might just as possibly be a simplification of Figure 22 as of Figure 20, though the Assyrian form is more clearly *outlined* in it.

I do not find the co-occurrence of palmettes and lotus flowers an anomaly, as some do. The Phœnician used the salient motives of his art-sources. The Egyptian lotus must therefore have been one of his most familiar units of design. The lotus blossoms ("lilies," "knops of flowers") might almost be part of the sacred tree, but the separate mention seems to indicate they were probably in a border above or below.

In the preceding section I pointed out the place in religious development that tree-worship occupied. The specialization of this out of the vaguer and more comprehensive betylae-worship (*bethelae*) marks a division of its scope. The formalization of sacred tree forms into mere mural ornamentation of stereotyped configuration marks a still later stage. In the centuries to which we are carried back by the earliest known Phœnician monuments, it is patent that the Phœnicians were no longer in a stage where their sole deities were rocks, trees, and pillars. These were thought of as images, local incarnations of a transcendent deity. Polytheism by the end of the Sidonian era was growing abstract, further removed from polydemonism; headed vaguely for the misty ideal of unity. Yet Phœnicia's scattered mode of living soon led this as yet tiny momentum toward abstraction to ally itself with the indifference that lack of intensity, concreteness and concentration incurred. The higher faith of her neighbors affected her not at all. So, although tree-worship was even at this time not unimportant in Egypt, and in the historic pedigree of Phœnicia's own Semitic past had played a great, if not a concretely and realistically pictured part, the sacred tree becomes for her workmen a mere ornamental stock-in-trade, most acceptable to tree-venerating customers. Hebrew tree-worship had been that common to all Canaan, bound up in the worship of betylae and ashera and groves. Artistic expression had been denied it, and by the time of the Temple when such artistic opportunity came, the content of the *symbol* had largely faded out of being. The decorative value appealed to the Tyrian architect and artisan, not the live significance; and it is doubtful if in this the Hebrews were much different. It was "groves" of *living* trees that meant something. The carved palm-trees on the walls, however, exhibited, museum-wise, another stage of Israelitish worship, a stage which even now existed in degenerate, specialized and perverted form in the near-by groves of Ashtoreth, those groves to which that heretical reversion to type so often brought unsteadfast Jews. The true faith of Yahveh had grown above it years ago.

VI.

The meaning of the word "cherubim" is doubtful; but the importance of the sacred beasts is hard to overestimate. The cherub persists throughout Hebrew history as the symbol or guardian of the holiest mysteries. Here in the Temple, we find cherubim on the walls and also (in the round) guarding the Ark of the Covenant in the Debir. As the cherub in the garden of Eden guarded the Tree of Life, so on the walls, carved Cherubim flanked the sacred trees.

The cherub seems to have been some kind of mythic griffin, composed of diverse traits chosen from well-known and respected animals. Lion characteristics, wings, "the face of a man," bull traits and features all seem to have fused in the ideal cherub. Probably, since fancy unchecked cannot keep stable, the cherub varied much from time to time. From a comparison of Isaiah i. 10 with Ezekiel x. 14, the algebraic cancellation of equals leaves the "face of a cherub" as the equivalent of that "of an ox." This I think was the predominant motive in the cherub.

If this be so, we are straightway again brought into that free exchange of ideals common throughout the Mediterranean basin. But first see what historic probability there is in the Hebrew race itself. The golden calf in the wilderness and the molten calves set up by Jeroboam in the Northern Kingdom so few years later (abolished by Josiah at Bethel in 640-609 B. C.) give good ground for believing the same symbol was not unknown between-times;— especially is this true since in both cases the worship seems naively to have been considered legitimate, to have been recognized as worship of Yahveh.

The notion has grown in late years that Yahveh was thought of as a bull-god in the original form of the nation's faith. In this case we have in the golden calf etc. another instance of that same reversion to type and primitive crudeness which the transcendentalists of Hebrew history always most bitterly combatted. It is not so much a mere example of primitive totemism as at first it seems. The bull-form had a spiritual reality at bottom. Israel was cradled, nurtured and educated to its maturity in the midst of bull-worshiping nations. It would be most unusual if this nation only should escape. The bull is the most natural emblem of generative force and sturdy strength to cattle-breeders, and such were all the half-Bedouin races of the Eastern Mediterranean.

The most obvious source of such a concept is Egyptian, the worship of the black Apis-bull of Osiris (Fig. 23), the so-called "bull of the West" who was considered as Osiris incarnate, and the worship of the white bull of Horus. The black Apis-bull was the answer to the demand that Hathor, the cow-goddess of the underworld, should have a masculine correlative to be complete. As a *cow*-goddess, she was stronger than Isis whose bovine partner was the Horus-bull. It is Hathor, the horned goddess with the sun-disk, who infers the existence of the bull of heaven, the bull-headed god

Fig. 23. BRONZE FIGURE OF APIS.
Wilkinson, *Ancient Egyptians*, Vol. I, p. 289.

most easily developed by the Hebrews into Yahveh, whose blood-cousin, though a black sheep of the family, was Moloch, also bull-horned.

In the Promised Land itself the influence of surrounding gods lent itself to the perpetuation of such an ideal. Not only was Moloch a bull-god,[18] but the Hittites also worshiped similar deities. In the remains of the mysterious Hittite palace at Euyuk there is a relief which shows a priest and priestess each with a hand lifted in adora-

[18] Cf. the Rabbis. Jarchi. on Jerem. vii. 31. Diodorus xx. 14.

tion to an image of a bull raised on a high pedestal with an altar before it.[86] Sandan, the Hittite Hercules, seems to have been considered as a bull-god.

Analogies multiply from all directions. Europa and the Zeus-bull, Ariadne and the Minotaur of Crete, Bacchus as a human-faced bull (Fig. 24); these on the Greek side via Crete and Mycenae with

Fig. 24. BACCHUS AS A HUMAN-FACED BULL.

Ohnefalsch-Richter, *Kypros, the Bible and Homer,* pl. CXCII, fig. 9.

a residuum of unmodified primitive characteristics, unite with the Assyrian winged and human-headed sacred bull on common footing.

Horned gods and horned demons occur in many religions. The horn is the symbol of power, of super-humanity. Kings adopt it for their crowns, professing divine right and descent. "Minos was bull-god as well as king. At certain feasts, and notably at his royal

Fig. 25. THE HERO GILGAMESH AND SACRED BULLS.

From the Chalcedony Seal as early as 3d millennium B. C. Ohne-falsch-Richter, *Kypros, the Bible and Homer.*

marriage, he wore a bull's mask, and his queen perhaps a cow's mask." The ruins of Cnossos are replete with horn-emblems and bull-masks. Legendary heroes and mythical demigods are adorned with horned caps or sprouting horns (cf. fig. 25). The Assyrian pantheon looks ridiculously like the stanchions of a well-stocked cattle-farm.

[86] W. J. Hamilton, *Researches in Asia Minor, Pontus and Armenia,* I, pp 393-395; Perrot and Chipiez, IV, 623, 656, 666, 672; L. Messerschmidt, *The Hittites,* pp. 42-50.

The bull-characteristics of the Cherub are the manifestation of Yahveh's own past.[97]

To the bull-form of the cherub were added wings. This likewise is a custom of long standing. In the very earliest strata of Cyprus, races which date from about 1000 to the middle of the sixth century B. C. (Græco-Phœnician) the juxtaposition of heraldic birds and holy trees or flowers is very frequent. They even seem some-

Fig. 26. VASE FROM KITION.
Ohnefalsch-Richter, *Kypros, the Bible and Homer*, pl. LXXIX.

times to be adoring a holy tree; perhaps holy birds were reared and kept in the grove of a divinity who was worshiped under the semblance of a natural or artificial tree. This finding of birds in the function of the later cherubim and guardian bulls of Assyria or in the position of Egyptian sphinxes (whose attitude toward the central pillar is purely decorative, shown by the generality of cases in which

[97] Gen. xlix. 24 seems to call Yahveh the Bull of Jacob.

the animals are back to back) makes the fusion of characteristics easy, once the character of their act is fused. Wings are the relics of such representations.

Figure 26 shows an interesting piece of Cyprian pottery of the earliest date where both beast and bird are adoring the ashera-tree (which also seems to be in a state of evolution into human form).

The taste for figures put face to face is Assyrian rather than Egyptian, and Phœnicia almost never chooses to place its mythic beasts in any but fronting poses. The famous Lion Gate at Mycenae is duplicated by numberless seals, paterae and glyptics. This is the position which has meaning; the other has none but ornamental intent. The flanking animals give prominence and impressiveness

Fig. 27. A PILLAR WITH GRIFFIN SUPPORTERS.

From Mycenae. Tsuntas, "Μυκῆναι," pl. V, fig. 6. Tsuntas and Manatt, *Myc. Age*, p. 254, fig. 131. Furtwangler, *Ant. Gemm.*, Vol. III, p. 44, fig. 18. Evans, *Myc. Tree and Pillar Cult*, p. 60, fig. 36.

to the ashera or pillar they support. Most of the detail on the betylae of Phœnicia is permeated by the inevitable and concomitant satellites, who are their watchdogs. The Egyptian sphinx and the Phœnician griffin (Fig. 27) merge with the Assyrian winged bull into the function of the cherub, and duplicate his known characteristics. The Assyrian bull is certainly the noblest and most dignified forefather the most "blue-stocking" cherub could long for. His calm majesty and massive power make him truly a fit guardian for any sacred Tree of Life. (Fig. 28.)

This brings me to a brief consideration of the symbolism of the cherub.

The undifferentiated pillar grew to be a pair, which each in turn specialized its sexual significance. The Ashera-pillar we found to have become phallic, answering the call of the all-mother, Astarte. The sacred tree on the walls of the temple manifests the development simple baetylic worship (exemplified in Jachin and Boaz) has reached on the feminine side. The masculine momentum towards

Fig. 28. WINGED BULL FROM KHORSABAD.
Perrot and Chipiez, *Babylonia and Assyria.*

phallicism does not in Semitic religion become over-frank or primary ; but it develops with much vigor in secondary or veiled forms. This the bull-worship seems to be. Baal-Peor,[98] the god of the Moabites and Midianites, seems to have enshrined this principle. Some scholars even go so far as to create out of the name Peor-Apis the Greek name Priapus. The Apis-bull soon came to be considered identical

* Numbers xxv. 1-2 etc.; Hosea ix. 16 etc.

with Baal, and Yahveh as *a* Baal must have held more than a modicum of this idea. In Phœnicia phallicism was attached to the sun-cult of Adonis-Tammuz and Isis-Ashtoreth-Venus. But the ideal of *strength* seems to have been the backbone of the deification. Masculinity does not imply sensuality—but develops the consideration of qualities such as reliability (cf. the covenant where Yahveh "abideth faithful"), war-power and physical strength. As such Yahveh need not be ashamed to own his symbol, the simple metaphor which these child people could easily visualize and understand.

VII.

Primitive religion is interesting more than for its own sake. Its intrinsic value must be in the contribution it makes to the philosophy of history. Every day of modern times makes the fact of evolution become more and more the fibre of our thought. But the wonder likewise grows. God even is content to let his children grow to knowledge of him through such imperfect visions of his reality as these we have been studying. The main thing is, they *grow*. And growth must be upward; and if upward, it is toward the perfection he has set as the ideal of perfect knowledge of him as Love. The ideal of a loving God is undreamed of in these dim ages, in the ideals the Temple embodied; brought from the desert wanderings to be spiritualized through stress and disappointment into Messianic hope, which even so did not hope for the Truth as Christ revealed it in our midst. We may not say, however, that this half-faith was valueless. In the eyes of the Lord, to whom "a thousand years are as a day, and a day as a thousand years," as being the promise of perfection, it was priceless. Israel was his chosen people. However near the wilderness the Temple may have stood, it faced the East where the dawn was breaking.

> "Well, you must know, there lies
> Something, the Curé says, that points to mysteries
> Above our grasp: a huge stone pillar, once upright,
> Now laid at length, half-lost, discreetly shunning sight
> I' the brush and brier, because of stories in the air—
> Hints what it signified, and why was stationed there,
> Once on a time. In vain the Curé tasked his lungs—
> Showed, in a preachment, how, at bottom of the rungs
> O' the ladder, Jacob saw, where heavenly angels stept
> Up and down, lay a stone which served him, while he slept,
> For pillow; when he woke, he set the same upright
> As pillar, and a-top poured oil: things requisite

To instruct posterity, there mounts from floor to roof
A staircase, earth to heaven: *And also put in proof*
When we have scaled the sky, we well may let alone
What raised us from the ground, and,—Paying to the stone
Proper respect, of course,—take staff and go our way,
Leaving the pagan night for Christian break of day.
. . . .
. . . .*Thus preached the Curé and no jot*
The more persuaded people but that, which once a thing
Meant and had right to mean, it still must mean. . . . .
. . . . Yon spire, you keep erect
Yonder, and pray beneath, is nothing, I suspect,
But just the symbol's *self* expressed in slate for rock,
Art's smooth for nature's rough, new chip from the old block!"*

* Robert Browning, "Fifine at the Fair," lines 2102-2119, 2125-8, 2152-5.

BIBLIOGRAPHY.

Alouf, Michael. *Baalbec.*

Anderson, R. E. *The Story of Extinct Civilisation.*

British Museum Catalogue of the Greek Coins of Cyprus.

Budge, E. A. W. *The Gods of the Egyptians.*

De Vogüè, *Le Temple de Jerusalem.*

Di Cesnola, A. P. *Salaminia.*
    Cyprus.

Donaldson. *Architectura Numismatica.*

Dulaure, J. A. *Des divinités generatrices.*

Engel. *Kypros,* II.

Evans, G. F. *Mycenean Tree-Cult.*

Fergusson, Jas. *The Temples of the Jews.*

Frazer, W. A, *Adonis, Attis, Osiris—Studies in Oriental Religion.*
    The Golden Bough.

Gerhard, F. "Ueber die Kunst der Phönicier," *Archäologische Abhandlungen.*

Griffith, F. Ll. *Archaeological Survey of Egypt.*

Howard, C. *Sex Worship.*

Hill, G. F. *Catalogue of Greek Coins of Lycaonia, Isauria and Cilicia.*

Jastrow. *Religion of Babylonia and Assyria.*

Knight, R. Payne. *Symbolism of the Ancients.*
    The Worship of Priapus in Ancient Times.

Langrange, M. S. *Etude sur les religions semitiques.*

Layard. *Monuments of Nineveh.*
    Culte de Venus.

Lenormant. *Musée des antiquités egyptiennes.*

Lenz, C. G. *Die Göttin von Paphos.*

Lepsius. *Denkmäler aus Aegypten.*

Maspero, O. *The Passing of the Empires* (Sayce edition).
    The Dawn of Civilization.
    The Struggle of the Nations.

Meursius. *Cyprus.*

Mosso. *The Palaces of Crete and their Builders.*

Muenter. F. *Der Tempel der himmlischen Göttin von Paphos.*

Murray, G. K. *The Rise of the Greek Epic.*

Ohnefalsch-Richter, Max. *Kypros, the Bible and Homer.*

Perrot and Chipiez. *History of Art in Antiquity:* "Ancient Egyptian Art," "Chaldea and Assyria," "Phœnicia and Cyprus," "Sardinia, Judea, etc.," "Greece."

Petrie, W. Flinders. *Egyptian Exploration Fund Reports.*

Place. *Ninivé et l'Assyrie.*

Prestel, J. *Die Baugeschichte des jüdischen Heiligthums.*

Ramsay. "Early Historical Relations Between Phrygia and Cappadocia," in *Journal of the Royal Asiatic Society*, XV.

Renan, E. *History of Israel* (Vol. II). *Mission de Phenicie* (Texte et Planches).

Shoebel. *La Mythe de la femme et la serpente.*

Smith, H. P. *Old Testament History.*

Smith, W. Robertson. *The Religion of the Semites.*

Stade, Siegfried. *Old Testament History.*

Stanley. *History of the Jewish Church.*

Trumbull, H. C. *The Threshold Covenant.*

Vellay. "Le dieu Thammuz," *Revue de l'histoire des religions* (1904) pp.154-162. *Le culte et les fêtes d'Adonis-Thammuz dans l'Orient antique.*

Walters. *British Museum Catalogue of Terra Cottas.*

Westropp and Wake. *Ancient Symbol Worship.*

Wolff, P. O. *Der Tempel von Jerusalem und seine Maasse.*

Also articles in:

Hasting's Bible Dictionary, s .v. Ashera, Astarte, Baal, Cherubim, Moloch, Osiris, Palm, Pomegranate, Solomon, Tammuz, The Temple.

Encyclopaedia Biblica, s. v. Temple, etc.

Jewish Encyclopedia, s. v. Temple, etc.

Writings of Herodotus, Athenaeus, Strabo, Pausanius, Diodorus Siculus, and Lucian (pseudo).

(The list might be prolonged indefinitely. I have put down only such books as were of actual and appreciable use to me in the preparation of this monograph.)